I0192173

The EDA Handbook for Middle Eastern Dance

Textbook

The EDA Handbook for Middle Eastern Dance

Textbook

By DaVid of Scandinavia

ISBN 978-0-6151-6681-0
Copyright © 2007 by David Badyal / The EDA

Author: David Badyal / DaVid of Scandinavia

Cover design: David Badyal
Cover photo: Annika Vallgren
Layout, typography & illustration: David Badyal
Photography by courtesy of performers and their photographers

First edition

I

Prologue

This handbook is dedicated to my instructors whom empowered me with the knowledge compiled here for you today. However, it could not have been possible without the ambition installed in me by my parents or without the tremendous support from my wife. And most of all, this handbook is dedicated to the dancers whom chose to invest their time, dedication and discipline under my tutelage. Without you, there would be no reason to write this handbook.

I would like to extend my gratitude to all the contributors to this handbook, without your hard work in the dance, help and generous support - this handbook would have remained incomplete.

Dance is a beautiful language of communication allowing dancers to express themselves in various ways, some find comfort in constructed styles and others find their home in culturally based styles. Either way, what we do embodies the gift of movement and lets us express our inner self in an at times more true manner than we may allow ourselves to do when we aren't dancing.

The purpose of this handbook is not to proclaim either world domination or superiority of the Egyptian Style of Raqs Sharki or Middle Eastern dance technique. Neither is it to devalue the hard work of thousands of dancers before me. This is a mere compilation of the knowledge we provide at the EDA that I have been handed down by my instructors, colleagues, sources of inspiration or through own experience.

The handbook provides an easy to understand reflection upon various subjects relevant to understanding the concepts we teach by at the EDA and relevant to dancers of any levels. Additional technique handbooks, as well as this guide, will provide an anatomic break down along with a detailed description of movements, concepts and guidelines of our stylization within the expression of Egyptian Raqs Sharki Technique as well as Middle Eastern Folklore. This handbook is not intended to replace

As dance is not a stagnant art form, neither is the ability to learn. In the light of this I already know that there will be updated editions, addendums and further development of this handbook in the future. There are numerous ways of approaching the Middle Eastern dance technique. This handbook is my approach as the dean of the EDA. If you find this handbook to be a valuable tool for you - respect it, respect me and respect the dance as your instructors as I respect my instructors and the dance. If you at any point should disagree with the approach used in this handbook or feel discomfort with the material - excuse my ignorance as a student as we are all life time students of this art form and together we keep on furthering it just like thousands have before us.

However, in order to progress within the EDA system of education within Middle Eastern dance, these are the principles and concepts expected to be installed and enforced by each and every dancer.

Bon Voyage,

DaVid of Scandinavia
Dean, the Ethnic Dance Academy
San Diego, California
August. 2007

Content

Chapter 6   *Layering Movements*

Chapter 7   *The Beauty of Choreography*

Chapter 8   *Improvisation*

Chapter 9   *The Hobbyist*

Chapter 10   *Taking it to the Next Level - The Professional Dancer*

Chapter 1   Introduction

Lesson 1.1   Anatomy

Proper knowledge of the body's muscle structure is an essential part of enabling yourself to increase body awareness and thus decrease the likelihood of injuries due to misplaced muscular focus and pressure. This chart is an introduction to the main muscles in the human body along with their Latin names and an outline of the anatomic illustration utilized in this handbook.

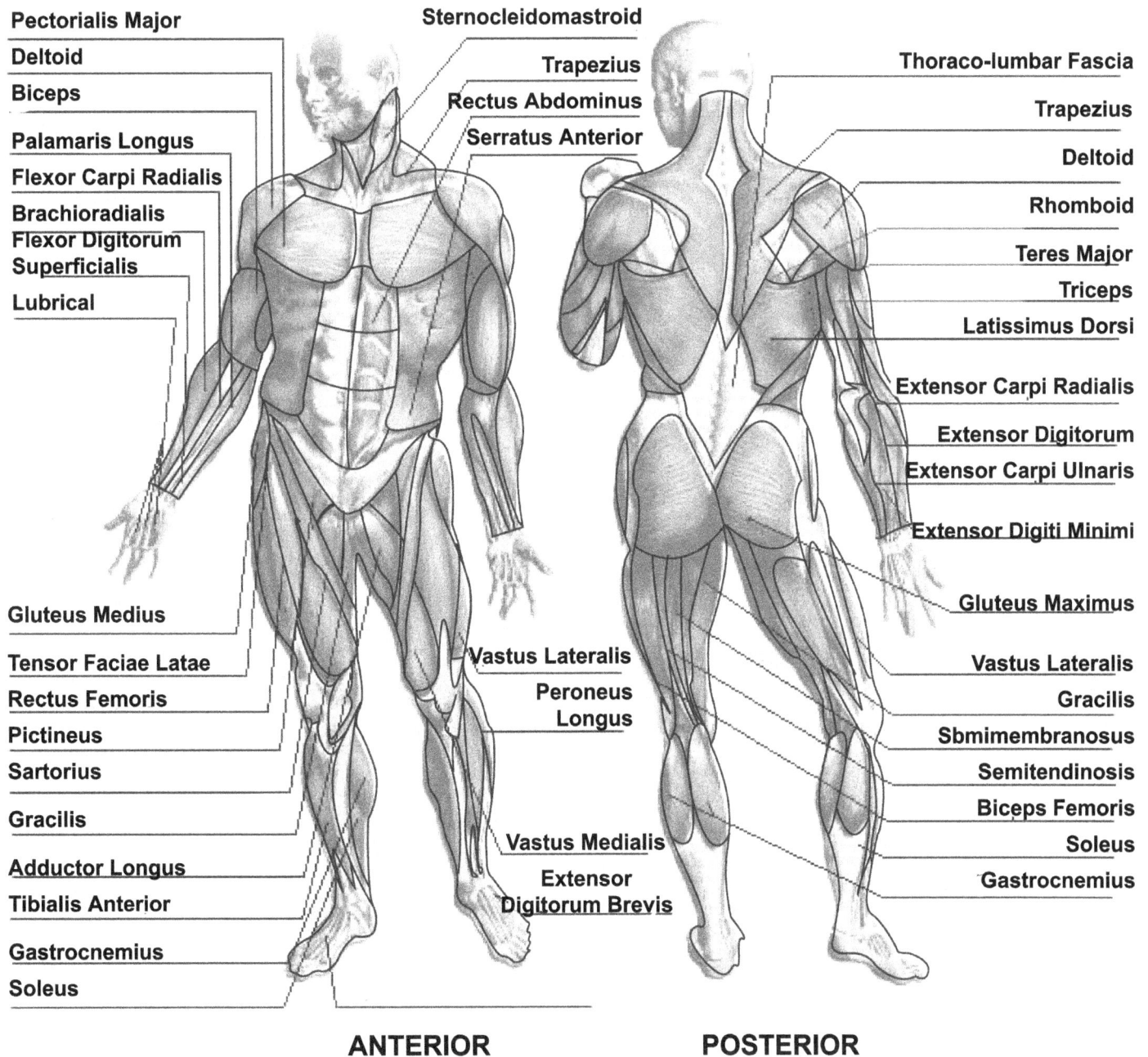

Pectorialis Major

Deltoid

Biceps

Palamaris Longus

Flexor Carpi Radialis

Brachioradialis

Flexor Digitorum Superficialis

Lubrical

Sternocleidomastroid

Trapezius

Rectus Abdominus

Serratus Anterior

Thoraco-lumbar Fascia

Trapezius

Deltoid

Rhomboid

Teres Major

Triceps

Latissimus Dorsi

Extensor Carpi Radialis

Extensor Digitorum

Extensor Carpi Ulnaris

Extensor Digiti Minimi

Gluteus Maximus

Gluteus Medius

Tensor Faciae Latae

Rectus Femoris

Pictineus

Sartorius

Gracilis

Adductor Longus

Tibialis Anterior

Gastrocnemius

Soleus

Vastus Lateralis

Peroneus Longus

Vastus Medialis

Extensor Digitorum Brevis

Vastus Lateralis

Gracilis

Sbmimembranosus

Semitendinosis

Biceps Femoris

Soleus

Gastrocnemius

ANTERIOR   **POSTERIOR**

Each muscle has a natural mechanical function, however - as dancers we are not studying the body as health workers, but as dancers. You will find an overview of the functions of the main muscle groups involved in Egyptian Raqs Sharki below starting with the Anterior and continuing with the Posterior.

Anterior muscle structure and functions
* Main groups engaged in dance

Muscle	Natural function	Dance function
* Sternocleidomastoid	Controls head motions	Head glides
Trapezius	Controls head motions	Neutral
* Deltoids	Raises and lowers the arm	Shoulder work
Pectorialis Major	Controls arm motions	Supports the arm when working in front of the body
Biceps	bends and extends the arm	Supports the arm when working above the head
Palmaris Longus Flexor Carpi Radialis	Bends and extends the wrist	Controls forearm and hand motions
* Flexor Digitorum Superficialis	Controls wrist motions	Controls the wrist - positions the wrist
* Lubrical	Controls the fingers	Controls finger movements and placements
* Rectus Abdominus	Supports the core and spine	Compensates against the back muscles Supports the core and spine, undulates, accents, supports leg movements
* Serratus Anterior	Supports the ribcage	Oblique accents Supports leg movements
* Gluteus Medius	Supports the hip and hip flexor	Helps contain hip movements
Tensor Faciae Latae	Bends and extends the knee	Supports accents
* Rectus Femoris	Bends and extends the knee	Pointing, extending the leg, holding the leg up, supports the leg, hip and leg accents
* Pectineus	Supports the core	Supports the core
* Gracilis	Supports the leg and core	Supports the leg and core
* Adductor Longus	Supports the leg and knee	Generates emphasis in hip accents, holds the leg in place
Vastus Medialis	Supports the knee	Supports the knee

Posterior muscle structure and functions
* Main groups engaged in the dance

Muscle	Natural Function	Dance function
* Thoraco-lumbar Fascia	Supports the spine	Supports the spine and lower back
		Elongates the lower back
		Releases the core
* Rhomboid	Support the arm	Chest work
* Triceps	Bends and extends the elbow/arm	Supports the arm
* Latissimus Dorsi	Supports the back, spine and arm	Supports the shoulder blade and arm
* Extensor Digitorum		
* Extensor Carpi Ulnatis		
* Extensor Digiti Minimi	Controls the forearm and wrist	Holds the wrist in place
Gluteus Maximus	Supports the leg, core and lower back	Neutral
* Semimembranosus	Supports the leg and knee	Generates all hip accents

Due to the fact that dancers relate to body parts by common names and not by their Latin names, here the anatomic sketch used in this handbook with the more general terminology. However, it is recommended to identify the most commonly used muscles on the anatomic sketch in Latin as well.

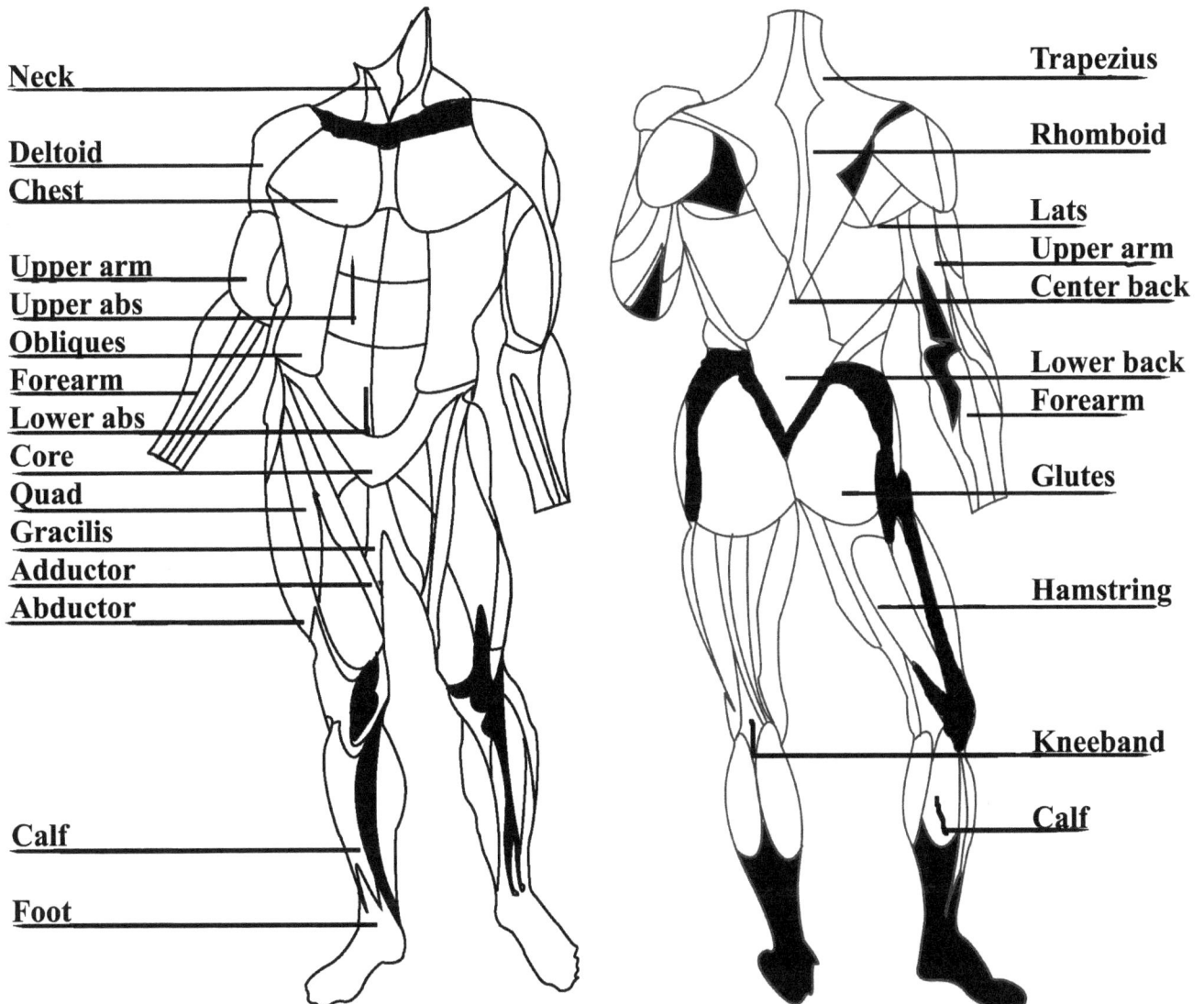

Neck
Deltoid
Chest
Upper arm
Upper abs
Obliques
Forearm
Lower abs
Core
Quad
Gracilis
Adductor
Abductor
Calf
Foot

Trapezius
Rhomboid
Lats
Upper arm
Center back
Lower back
Forearm
Glutes
Hamstring
Kneeband
Calf

13

Lesson 1.2 Injury Prevention

Several things play a significant part in a long lasting dance career, but one of the most important however is injury prevention. Too many dancers suffer from injuries at various times in their dance careers, injuries that could easily have been prevented through consistently paying attention to the following;
1.   Posture
2.   Technique
3.   Warm-ups, stretches, flexibility and cool-downs
4.   Muscle awareness, muscle memory and strength

Correct posture

One of the most common causes of injury within Raqs Sharki comes from bad habits with posture or from the dancer's posture getting lazy after some time in the dance. Injuries such as lower back pain, sprains and inflammations are, sadly, often caused through lack of attention to correct posture.

In order to understand the concept of posture, one has to look at the anatomic build up of the body as well as the axis of alignment when one dances. There are a few general rules when it comes to dance posture;
1. Muscles are engaged at all times - even when "relaxed".
2. Joints are always soft and flexible.
3. The core is engaged at all times.

Frontal alignment grid and axis
1 & 2. Shows the alignment axis.
3.   Shows the alignment of the feet and heels.
4.   Even knees.
5.   Square hips.
6.   Contracted center back and diaphragm (aligns with #4).
7.   Square shoulders

Weight alignment on feet - flat
1. Primary weight point in ball of foot
2. Secondary weight point in ball of foot
3. Weight point in heel evening out the weight on ball and heel in the foot.

Weight alignment on feet - relevé
1. Primary support in ball of foot supported by calves and ankles

Tip: A great way of avoiding sprained ankles is to do calf killers prior to engaging in dance activities.

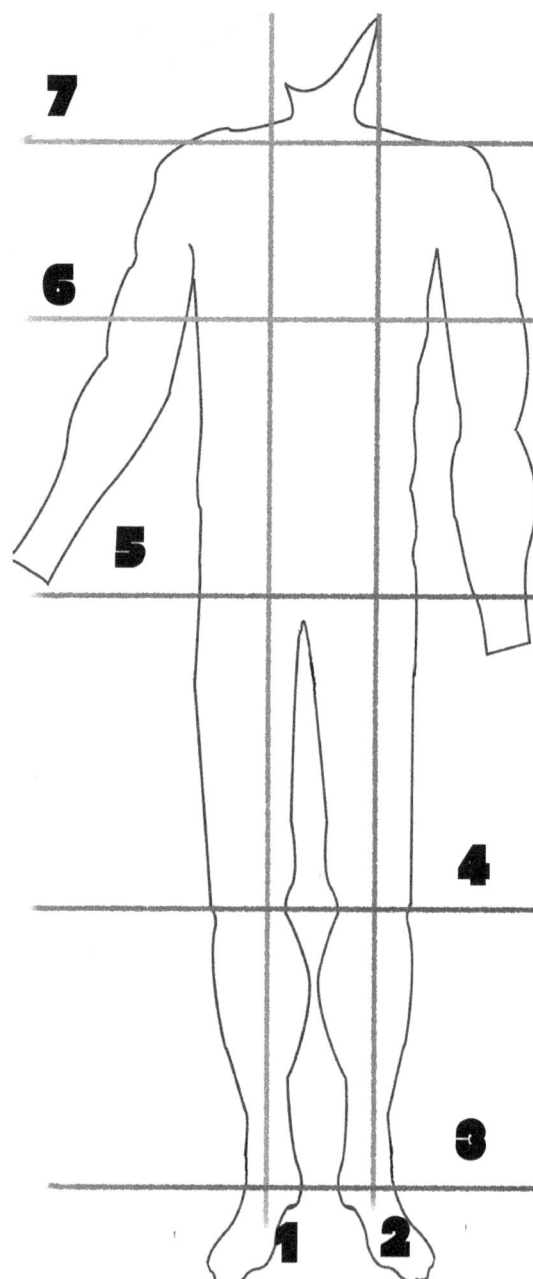

The vertical lines through the illustrations to the right demonstrate the body alignment while the gray areas on the illustrations to the left demonstrate what muscle groups are engaged to maintain the posture.

Profile alignment axis

The center of each body part is aligned when viewing the posture alignment in profile in neutral. Center feet, calves, thighs, hips, chest and neck should be aligned and the weight should be even when working in neutral (ideal everyday posture).
The ankle, knee and hip joints are engaged, soft and flexible.

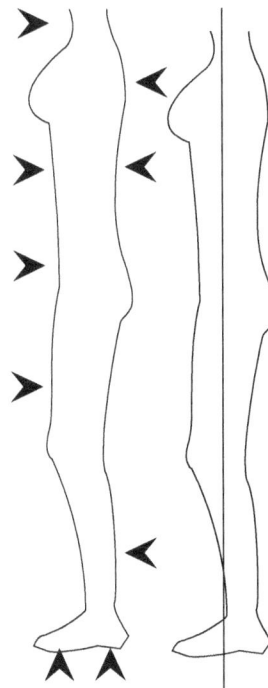

Profile alignment axis - folklore

Notice how the angles in the body are excaudated in the folklore posture; The weight remains even on the feet, but the knee joints bend forwards as the hip joint bends backwards and compensate each others angles. The dancer should feel a pull downwards to the floor in the core providing a grounded and strong expression in the posture.

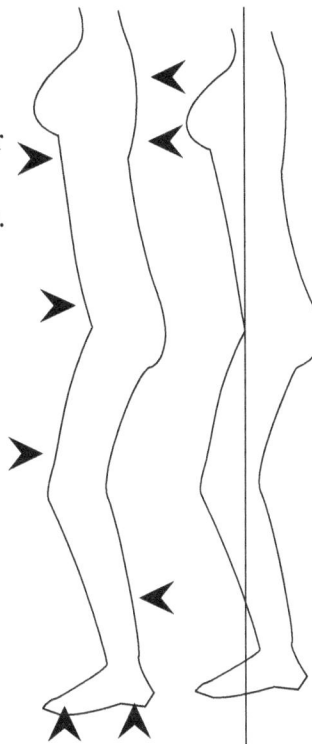

Profile alignment axis - relevé

As Middle Eastern folklore often is danced in relevé, the posture in this position gives essential knowledge of how to execute the movements when dancing in relevé.

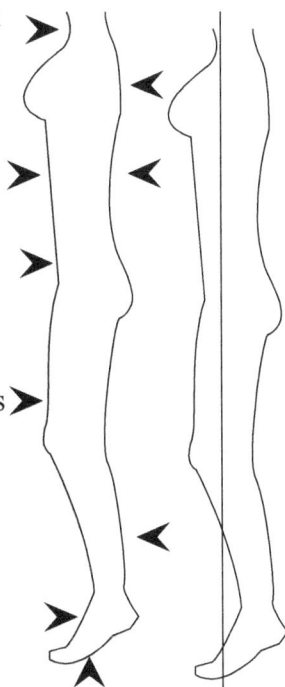

Strengthening the core is an essential part of being able to keep posture. Everyday exercises focusing on the abdomen and back make a significant difference in how successful the dancer is in maintaining the core and posture while dancing.

The further the dancer bends into a movement or stylization, the more extreme these angles will become in order to correctly distribute weight and maintain the axis of alignment.

Understanding this concept of compensation is the key to successfully preventing injuries when executing movements. These rules of compensation are always maintained, no matter how upright the stylization of the dance may be.

Correct technique

Correct technique is reflected in the articulation and the visual outcome of a movement. It also shows how well you as a dancer have understood and absorbed the concept of the movement. Maintaining the weight compensation in your posture in the movement comes first. Second is the concept of the movement itself along with proper muscle engagement. Correct execution and compensation in a movement will effectively strengthen and condition a dancer's body, as well as help avoiding injuries that may be detrimental to a dance career. Paying specific attention to given technical explanation enhances the body awareness and will help making the technique crisp, strong and accurate. A good recommendation is to keep a notebook or a text file with personal notes to keep track of tips and tricks beneficial to one's personal perception of the technique. When progressing dancers will eventually have a reference register where they can backtrack and re-discover various finesses in the technique to keep on challenging themselves. This is a very helpful tool especially with isolations and localizing the muscles involved various layer combinations.

Warm-ups, stretches, flexibility and cool-downs

Warm-ups prepare the body for the impact of the workout to come. The goal of the warm-ups is to increase the bloodstream through the muscles with extra focus on the main muscle groups that will be engaging in the workout / rehearsal / practice. For Raqs Sharki these muscle groups would be the core (back and front), shoulders, arms and thighs. Through warm-ups one avoids impacting a cold muscle and thus spraining it. Injuries caused by lack of warm-ups are long lasting and should be avoided as much as possible.

Stretches increase the flexibility of the muscles after the impact of a workout. As a dancer, flexibility is one of the key qualities enabling the dancer to move the way needed to in order to execute the movements. Stretches preserves flexibility and elasticity in the muscle. Proper stretches will also decrease the soreness after a workout session. The perk of stretching is that the muscles will not only remain flexible and elastic, but they will also pump up better during a workout - and in the long run gain size as well as become more flexible. The goal along with stretches is to wind down the body after the impact of the workout - called cool-downs. Basically, this refers to stabilizing the pulse and for the body to calm down after the physical activity just completed.

Muscle awareness, muscle memory and strength

Any part of a workout - be it warm-ups, the main session, or the stretches and cool-downs - increase muscle awareness. This term refers to the ability of localizing, engaging and being aware of a muscle while dancing. The more muscle awareness a dancer has, the more likely he or she is to master various layer combinations as well as grasp the nuances in different ways to execute a movement.

Repetitive motion builds muscle memory. This means that the muscles will recognize and remember certain combinations of "duties" given to them after having repeated them a certain amount of times previously. Science dictates that in order to create muscle memory, one has to keep doing the same movement/combination for 8 minutes and "man could you save yourself a lot of time" by investing those 8 minutes focused already the first time when learning something new and avoid bad habits. Muscle memory is also the motivation for drills in classes where certain movements or combinations are drilled over and over again.

DaVid of Scandinavia

Getting used to the movement and get comfortable with it is the first step in the right direction. The second is catching mistakes immediately. Third is to take corrections from the instructor to become more aware of the specifics of a movement and increase body awareness.

Strengthening the muscles is a great way of increasing muscle awareness and become stronger in the technique and more confident in it's execution. The most important benefit, however, is gaining more control over the movements and decrease the likelihood of injuries greatly through stronger muscles - a subject addressed later in this handbook.

Lesson 1.3 Rhythms

The EDA bases its philosophy of Middle Eastern dance around authentic expression and strong musicality. In order to express these qualities properly it is important to understand the structure of Middle Eastern music and rhythms. The following is an introduction to the basic structure of the most common rhythm patterns used in Middle Eastern music where D (dum) acts as the base and T (tek / teke) acts as the treble in the rhythm patterns. These rhythms may of course be elaborated at the musicians' discretion, but this is an introduction to the basics.

Saiidi
Saiidi is a 4/4 rhythm and is characteristic for music from Upper Egypt (south):

1 2   3   4
D T | DD T
Dum Tek Dum Dum Tek

Masmoudi (Balady)
Masmoudi is a 4/4 rhythm:

1   2   3   4
DD | T | D | TT
Dum Dum Tek(-e-tack) Dum Tek(-e-TekTek-e)

Here demonstrated with the Zagat pattern for the rhythm known to dancers as Balady in brackets.

Maqsoum
Maqsoum is a 4/4 rhythm:

 1   234
D | T D T
Dum Tek-e-tack-tack Dum Tek-e-tack

Malfouf
Malfouf is a 4/4 rhythm:
 1   2
D T | T
Dum Tek Tek

Lilla Varese

Fallahi

Fallahi is a 2/4 rhythm. Fellahi means farmer or person from the countryside:

1   2

D T | T D T

Dum Tek Tek Dum Tek

Zaar

Zaar is a 2/4 rhythm and is characteristic for exorcisms:

1   2

D T D T

Dum Tek Dum Tek

Ayub

Ayub is a 3/4 rhythm:

1 2   3

D T D T

Dum Tek Dum Tek

Zaffa

Zaffa is a 4/4 rhythm characteristic for wedding processions:

1   2   3 4

D T D T D TT

Dum Tek Dum Tek Dum Tek Tek

Samaii

Samaii is a 10/8 rhythm and is characteristic for Anadalusian music:

1 2 3 4 5 6 7 8 9 10

D | | T | | DD | T

Dum Tek Dum Dum Tek

Khaleegi

Khaleegi is a 4/4 rhythm and is characteristic of music from
the Persian Gulf area:

1 2 3   4

D T D TT

Dum Tek Dum Tek Tek

The important fact to realize about Middle Eastern rhythms is the significant difference in structure compared to western music. Quite a few of the beats are in between the count as you can see, therefore it is necessary to learn to identify the rhythm patterns themselves and not just count the base beats when addressing the rhythm in a music piece.

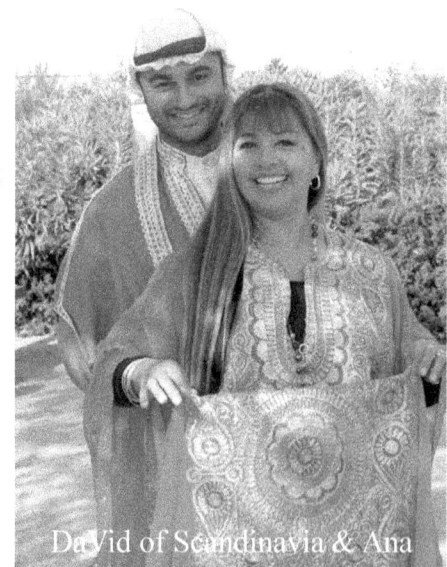

David of Scandinavia & Ana

Lesson 1.4   Blocking

The concept of blocking is frequently utilized in established dance styles. Basically it means to group counts together to make it easier to remember dance material. At the EDA we work by 6 different concepts of blocking:

1. Technical count
2. Movement count
3. Sequence count
4. Rhythmic count
5. Musical/Lyrical count
6. Breath count

It may seem confusing in the beginning to relate to these terms, but the logic is as follows;

1. Technical count

    Refers to the count a movement is build up by. Each count refers to a certain part of the movement at a certain place/time in the movement. This ensures consistency in the technique and makes it easier to identify where in the technical count layering occurs. Also, technical count enables the dancer to synchronize various counts in different layers together.

2. Movement count

    Refers to groups of technical counts and makes it easier to count numbers of movements in a sequence. Choreographies at the EDA are usually written in movement count in black.

3. Sequence count

    Refers to groups of movement counts and makes it easier to block out sequences in repetitions. Repetitions ensure familiarity with the material both for the dancer and the audience. Choreographies at the EDA are usually written with sequence counts in gray.

4. Rhythmic count

    Refers to the rhythmic count as presented in the previous lesson. This ensures accuracy in the dancer's technique and movements when it comes to following the rhythmic image of the music.

5. Musical/Lyrical count

    Refers to the lyrical image of the music and ensures accuracy in the dancer's expression and timing.

6. Breath count

    Refers to the count of movements or sequences that fit on a full breath, an inhale or an exhale. The breath should at all times remain calm and controlled and thereby provide a second nature count to the dancer. Mastering this concept provides extensive consistency in a dancer's work.

Lesson 1.5   Layering

One of the main basic principles of Middle Eastern dance is layering. Layering is the technical term for combining isolated movements and executing them at the same time. This seems to be the more challenging part of Middle Eastern dance technique, however, mastering the concept of layering enables the dancer to reflect a more consistent and accurate presentation of the musical image and curve in the music.

According to the EDA the way to master the concept of layering is through allowing each movement to reside in specific muscles and body parts - or more academically called body awareness and isolation. Thus, when the dancer executes isolated movements together - each body part will have specific chores to execute.

Example:

Shimmy	generated from the hamstrings
with counter clockwise Ummi	generated from the obliques
with counter clockwise chest circle	generated from the rhomboids and lats
with horizontal snake arms	generated from the lats, triceps, biceps, forearms and wrists

This combination of movements will in addition give the illusion of the following movements:
- Abdominal undulation
- lateral body wave
- Zaar characteristics

So just for the curiosity of it, and being meticulous, one could divide layers into categories as follows:

1. Rhythmic layer
   - reflects the rhythm
2. Lyrical layer
   - reflects the lyrics
3. Melodic layer
   - reflects the melody line
4. Stylistic layer
   - reflects the style of the dance

The complexity of Middle Eastern music requires dancers to tune their ears to these aspects of the music and the dance. The EDA also works by a prioritization concept when it comes to layering. Each layer has a priority reflecting the priority of the sound the layer is visualizing to the viewer. Let's illustrate this by using the layering example above.

Example:

The musical image consists of the instruments darbouka, kanoon, violins and keyboard. This occurs in an instrumental part in the musical piece in question and the instruments and layers of movement are prioritized in the following order:

1. Kanoon	Shimmy	
2. Keyboard	counter clockwise Ummi and chest circle	
3. Violins	horizontal snake arms	
4. Darbouka	basic beat and emphasis	

There are no limits to how detailed one may be when reflecting the music. However, this is where the rule of visibility and perception steps in;

> *"Dance is a performance art form. If a movement isn't clearly articulated and/or is not visible and the viewer can not perceive or see the movement - the dancer isn't doing it." DaVid*

Basically this means that all movements have to be clearly articulated and have a visual role in the combination of layers or sequence in order to be "valid". This rule is applicable to all prioritization of layers.

Lesson 1.6   Terminology

The EDA and this handbook focuses it's terminology upon common concepts and names utilized for movements and movement concepts in the Egyptian style of Middle Eastern dance according to the stylization by Mahmoud Reda, Ballet terminology, references to inventors/sources of movement concepts and references to stylistic characteristics.

Lesson 1.7   Stylization and Technique

Stylization are recognizable trademarks in a discipline such as positioning of the body, positioning of arms, legs and feet. The EDA and this handbook bases it's stylization and technique upon recognized and acclaimed representatives of the style, the Reda Troupe, The Kaumayya Troupe, Egyptian Folklore, Ballet and instructors as listed in the reference library in this book.

Lesson 1.8   Ballet Theory and Terminology

As a newly introduced student to the stylized and refined methodology of Middle Eastern dance one may ask why Ballet theory and terminology is brought into the concepts of Middle Eastern dance. The answer is simple: the most stylized and structured dance technique available today is Ballet. And, Mahmoud Reda, whom stylized the Egyptian expression of Middle Eastern dance, also utilized concepts from Ballet to uniform the expression of the style. Further, when taking a look at various line and folkdances from the Middle East one will see that there are very clear lines between the dances as stylized for stage and performance work and Ballet. As accuracy and structure enables a dancer to portray a vision to a musical piece more precisely - it is a simple task to comprehend the necessity of Ballet theory and terminology in Middle Eastern dance.

According to the EDA and this handbook there are some slight modifications to the basic concepts of Ballet utilized in Middle Eastern dance. Following are the most commonly utilized terms and concepts along with the modifications as according to the EDA.

Modification to basic posture:
Ballet supports the posture through the inside of the legs, the core, the diaphragm, the upper back and the chest. The legs and the torso kept at a strict vertical position. Here compared with the neutral posture of Middle Eastern dance.

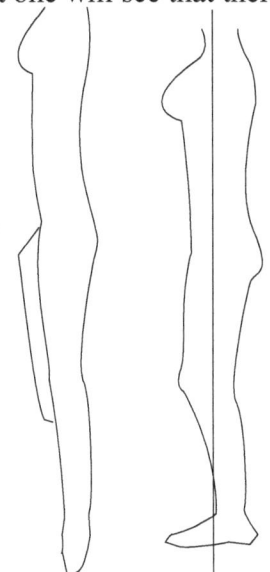

The modification to this for Middle Eastern dance according to this handbook is as follows:
The knees remain soft and flexible at all times and the posture is supported through the muscle groups as outlined in the illustration.

This handbook makes use of the same positions of the feet as Ballet. The slight modification is that instead of the linear position of the feet in Ballet, all foot positions are at a 90 degree angle placing the feet facing diagonally between 10 and 11, and 1 and 2 oclock beneath the core and hip.

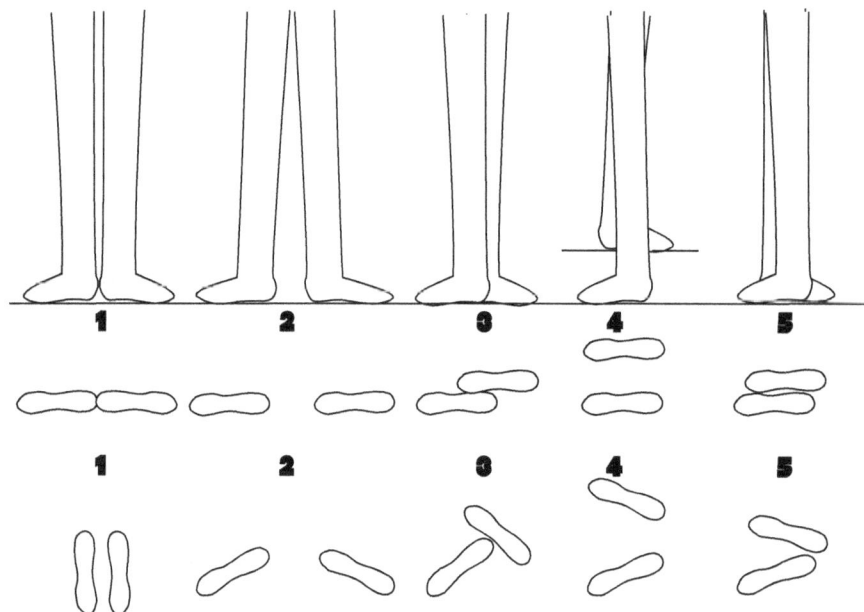

Positions of the feet in Ballet (top) and Middle Eastern dance:
(1) 1. position (2) 2. position (3) 3. position (4) 4. position (5) 5. position

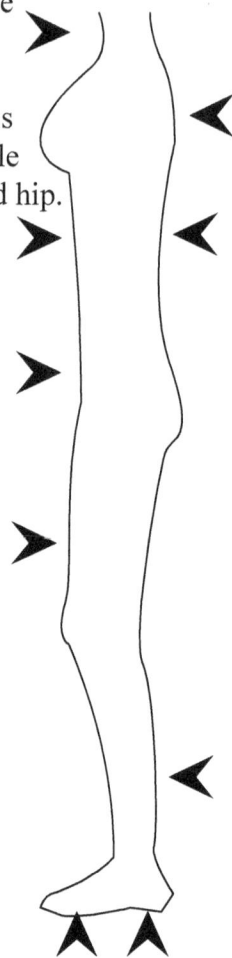

The following Ballet terms are utilized with a liberal interpretation of the movement and/or concept in question with the EDA abbreviation in parenthesis;

Arabesque	(A) extension of the leg, creating an extension from the finger tips to the toes
Bras, positions des	(#) positions of the arms
Chassé	chased, A 3 count step where one foot chases the other (horse step / triplets)
Choreographer	Composer or inventor of dances
Choreography	the actual steps, grouping and patterns of a dance composition
Corps, positions des	(PdC) positions of the body
Croisé	(cross) crossing of the legs/thighs
Demi point	(relevé) half toe/point
Demi plié	(folklore) half bend of the knees
Demi tour	(DT) half turn
Derrière	back
Devant	front
Double	(D) double
Entré	entrance
Étendu	(É) outstretched, extended
Finale	final section of a dance composition

22

Jambe	(*) leg
Labanotation	dance notation system invented by Rudolf Von Laban, developed and perfected by the Dance Notation Bureau, NY
Mains, positions des	(pdM) positions of the hands
Notation	a system of recording dance compositions in writing - dance notation. The EDA operates by it's own constructed dance notation system - the EDA Dance Notation System, EDA DNS™.
Opposition	(O) engaging and activating diagonal body parts in a sequence
Pas de Bourrée	(PdB) bourrées are usually tiny running steps in which the feet are kept close together. They are most often performed in relevée and can travel in any direction
Pas de Deux	(PdD) dance for two
Passé	passed, the foot of one leg passes the knee of the supporting leg
Pieds, Positions des	(PdP) positions of the feet
Pirouette	(P) whirl/spin with spotting
Plat, à	flat (on the feet)
Port de Bras	(Pd#) arm paths
Quatrième, À la	(4th) fourth position Ballet of the body
Relevé	(Rel) raised
Repetition	rehearsal/repeat/practice
Rond	round/circular
Rond de Bras	(RdB) circular motion of the arms
Rond de Jambe	(RdJ) circular motion of the leg
Seconde, À la	(2nd) second position Ballet of the body
Spotting	(Sp) movement of the head/eyes in turns. The head is the last to leave and first to arrive at the focal point chosen. Often use to prevent dizziness
Step	transition of weight from one leg to the other
Stretching	loosening, limbering of the muscles. Détiré
Supporting leg	versus working leg. The supporting leg supports the body and initiates a movement while the working leg is freed up to execute given movement
Tour	(T) turn
Turn-out	(TO) the ability of the dancer to turn feet and legs out from the hip joints to a 90 degree position - en-dehors
Warm-up	exercise done to prevent injuries in muscles and tendons and to prepare for strenuous activity
Working leg	(active leg) executes movements

4th   2nd

Lesson 1.9 Borrowed Terminology from other Styles

The EDA Middle Eastern technical terminology borrows concepts and terms from other styles such as Flamenco, Kathak, Bharata Natyam, Jazz and Hiphop.

Lesson 1.10 Folklore

Being that the Middle Eastern dances are based upon folkloric dances from the various Middle Eastern countries, it is a given that in order to achieve a through understanding for the dances of these countries - one has to study the folkloric dances of the country in question. One may question why folklore is given such a prominent position. The answer is simple; to do a representable presentation of Middle Eastern dances, which are based upon cultural folkloric dances, it is not enough just to learn the end product. The dancer has to know where the movement comes from, how it has developed, how it has been stylized and what its characteristics are in order to give room for a personal expression within the style - while still preserving the style. The dancer has to know the rules of the dance styles in order to chose between abiding by them or breaking them.

Mahmoud Reda revolutionized the Egyptian folklore through stylizing the dances while preserving their characteristics. While this handbook dedicates a whole chapter to the significant eras, names and personas in the dance; it is enough to say that most dancers today can trace their pedigree and lineage back to Mahmoud Reda.

Characteristics of Egyptian folklore are large organic movements, grounded posture and loosely contained movement patterns along with chest work, shoulder work, heel bounces and hip work.

Lesson 1.11 Raqs Sharki

The Egyptian style of Raqs Sharki as we know it today has developed from the folkloric dances of Egypt, bringing along a long tradition of dance, culture and music with it. There are set rules and regulations for how an Egyptian Raqs Sharki performance is conducted and for how the dancer is expected to move as well as behave

Characteristics for Egyptian Raqs Sharki are intricate accented and organic movements, level changes, contained movement patterns, chest work, arm work, shoulder work, abdominal work, leg work, hip work and intricate visualization of the musical image as presented to the dancer.

Siw Øksnes

Lesson 1.12 A Brief History Lesson

The Egyptian style, or Raqs Sharki minn Misr in Arabic, as we know it today is directly based on Mr. Mahmoud Reda's work to stylize and refine Egyptian folklore and the Egyptian Raqs Sharki. But let us go back further in time to the time before Mr. Reda.

There is no clear documentation stating where and how Raqs Sharki evolved, but what we do know for sure is that the concept of Raqs Sharki as we know it today started out with the times when the Western world discovered "Bellydance" in the Middle East and Turkey and brought it to Hollywood. Hollywood introduced the two piece costumes known as Bedlah and as a direct result of this - the Egyptian entertainment industry adopted the costuming out of commercial interest. Names such as Naema Akef, Taheya Carioca and Samia Gamaal made the Bedlah a part of their performances as well as the veil which was also imported from Hollywood. Being the Paris of the Middle Eastern world - Cairo was up-to-date on costuming, hair, makeup, and also creativity within the dance. Influences from the musicals from Hollywood had great impact on the presentation and movements of Raqs Sharki in the black/white era of Egyptian movies. Famous writers and composers such as Farid Al-Atrache and Abdul Halim Hafez wrote musical pieces that still are considered to be top notch dance material. The dancing was based on traditional Egyptian folklore dances and Raqs Sharki. This time period is often referred to as the Golden Era.

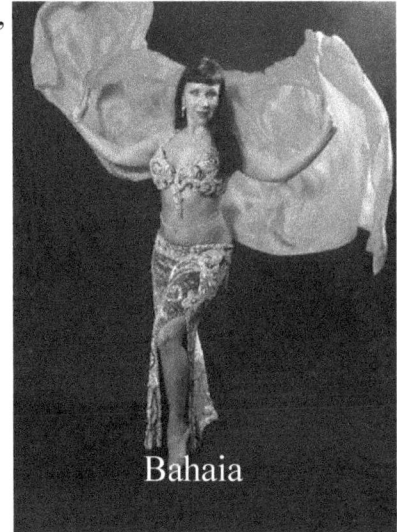

Bahaia

Times evolved and so did technology - color TV was introduced. Nagwa Fouad known as the queen of Egyptian Raqs Sharki was the star in the Egyptian movies. Nagwa's presentation was more glamorous, technically more nuanced, and more commercial and movements became more articulated as the 60s and 70s hit Egypt.

This is also the time period where Fifi Abdou was introduced to the scene. The girl from Alexandria that went to Cairo and became one of the greatest most sought after stars in Egyptian Raqs Sharki history - and still is. Fifi Abdou's personal background and style of dancing made the general audience worship her as an icon. Fifi is therefore known as the dancer of the people - the Shaabiya. She has supported a band of 35 musicians and singers - and their families - throughout her career. She is probably one of the highest priced dancers today and her shows last for 2 hours. Fifi Abdou is today one of the wealthiest women in Egypt. Her famous quote "I have learned to read and write and also speak English. I have no university degrees, but I have a doctorate from the biggest university...the university of life" and extensive work to help the poor and underprivileged in Cairo has made her even more popular.

Fifi Abdou

Another prominent name of this Era was Suheir Zaki. This excellent dancer is not only known for her extraordinary dance capabilities, but also for being the first dancer to ever dance to Oum Koulthoum's music, the mother of classical Arabic song tradition. With Oum Koulthoum's personal approval and blessing - Suhair's interpretation of Oum Kolthoum's songs still sets the standard for how a true Egyptian style dancer should address these treasures of music. Suheir Zaki is often referred to as the pure dancer.

As Nagwa Fouad, Fifi Abdou and Suhair Zaki reached fame and glory though their shows, TV performances and parts in the movies another important and significant thing was happening. Mr. Mahmoud Reda - an Olympic level gymnast - started the first Egyptian Folklore troupe in 1959 after having traveled all over Egypt documenting the characteristics of folkdances of his country. Mahmoud Reda drew from techniques of Jazz, Russian Ballet, Russian Character dance and Indian dances. This was a milestone in the history of Egyptian dances. Mr. Reda stylized and presented the Egyptian folkdances on large stages with his dancers - the Reda Band with Farida Fahmy as the principal dancer. This later evolved into the world famous Reda Troupe.

The Reda troupe weren't only different in the way that they incorporated classical dance techniques such as Ballet and Russian Character dance into the Egyptian folklore dances. They were educated college graduates that dedicated themselves to the Egyptian folklore were as dancers previously often had been of less fortunate social backgrounds.

The Reda Troupe toured not only in Egypt but throughout 58 countries all over the world. Thanks to Mr. Mahmoud Reda choreographers and performers such as Farida Fahmy, Aida Nour, Raqia Hassan, Dina, Mo Geddawi, Yousri Sharif, Ahmed Fekry, Magdy El-Leisy, Mohamed Shahin and Methat Fahmy are still carrying on the legacy of the Egyptian Folklore and Raqs Sharki dances.

As the Reda Folklore reached more and more people and the Reda School received recognition all over the world - the prestige of being a Reda dancer increased. Most dancers we see today have Reda background in one way or another.

Yousry Sharif

Speaking of which, Dina is probably the most famous Egyptian dancer both in and out of the Arab world with Reda background. Aside from her rather daring costume choices, she is also one of the most well educated dancers on the scene today. Starting out with the Reda Troupe, Dina soon moved on to the commercial stages and soon became one of the most sought after stars during the 1980s, and still is.

In reference to the recent stars of the Raqs Sharki sky of Cairo names such as Randa Kamal, Dandash, Nour, Yasmina of Cairo, Soraya, Camelia - and the list could go on and on - all have the Reda name in their pedigree either through having been a part of the Reda School itself or through studying with one of the many many recognized choreographers and performers that are connected to the Reda name.

Raqia Hassan was also the first to organize an annual Middle Eastern Dance festival in Cairo by the name of Ahlan Wa Sahlan, a very successful venture indeed frequented by thousands of eager dancers every year. Aida Nour now also organizes several festivals a year for dancers with a well of knowledge offered through the instructors. Performers, instructors and choreographers highly respected and awed for their work such as Sahra Saeeda, Zahra Zuhair, Jillina, Aziza, Bahaia, Suzanne Petren Abou Shebika, Majken Wærdahl and Hilde Lund to mention a few, but not even close to the numerous dancers that are directly connected to the Reda Troupe members. Lucy is also a

Hilde Lund

significant performer and instructor on the Egyptian scene. Her highly trained and nuanced dance style has inspired dancers all over the world to keep on working at it. She is often referred to as the Queen of Balady - due to her high quality interpretations of the music.

Another group that has had significant impact on the dance scene is the Egyptian National Folkloric troupe - with members such as Lubna Emam and Faten Salama - this troupe has toured all over the world with long engagements in the Khaleeg area as well as other parts of the world.

The EDA divides the Egyptian stylization and technique into 3 main groups;
- Pre-Reda (Old Skool - more folklore influenced)
- Reda (more stylized and Ballet influenced)
- Contemporary (New School - western influenced through Jazz, Modern Ballet, Hip Hop etc.)

Lesson 1.13 Egyptian Raqs Sharki Worldwide

As Egyptian Raqs Sharki has spread worldwide and intercepted with other dance styles - specific characteristics of Egyptian Raqs Sharki have developed in different parts of the world. Influences from other dance styles and movement philosophies have been incorporated - providing new and exciting expressions of the style.

Chapter 2   The Basic Concepts of Raqs Sharki

Lesson 2.1   Positioning of Arms and Feet

Stylistic consistency is one of the traits of an EDA trained dancer. One of the essentials in this stylization is strict positioning of the arms and feet. The EDA format of arm positioning is based on 8 positions defined by the incision point of the wrist in the circle of the arm and horizontal lines from the following points:

1. the center of the hip joint
2. the top of the hip bone
3. the waist line
4. the diaphragm
5. the chest line
6. the eyes
7. the top of the head
8. above the head at same width as position 1.

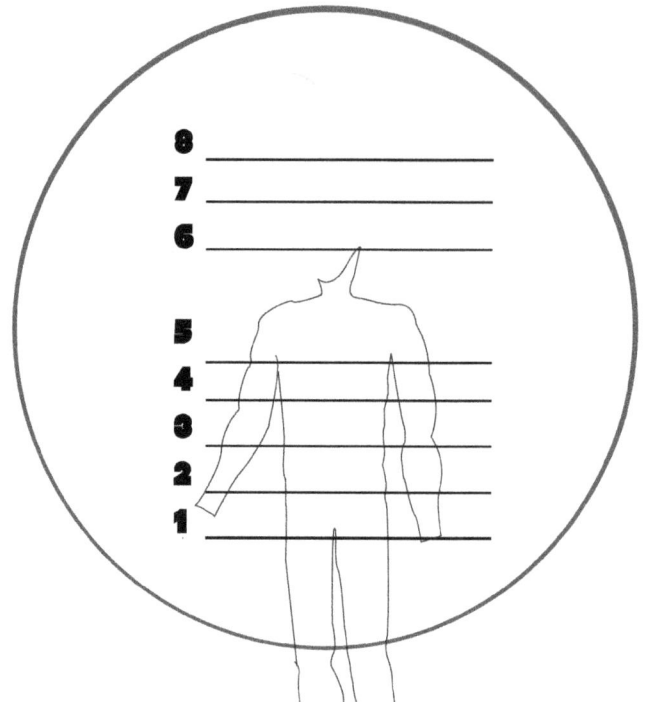

The arms are activated through engaging the lats and triceps - pulling the elbow diagonally outwards from the body creating a negative space between the body and the arm. There is an extension present from the lats to the tip of the middle finger and the elbow remains flexible and the weight of the arm rests on the lats at all times. This provides the movements with room for execution without the arms getting in the way. Arms are positioned according to the outlined curve below.

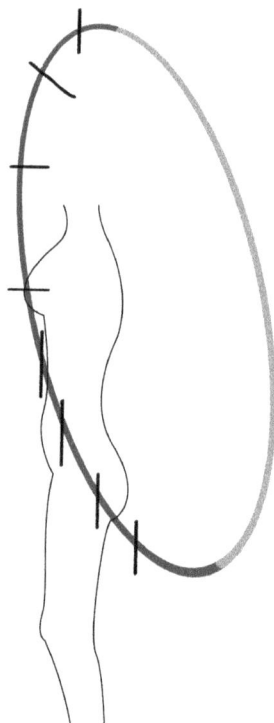

The positioning of the feet doesn't only prevent serious injuries but also impacts the visual outcome of a movement. Below are the Ballet foot placement positions as adapted by the EDA for Middle Eastern Dance. The turnout is generated by rotating the hip joint and squeezing forwards from the inner thigh.

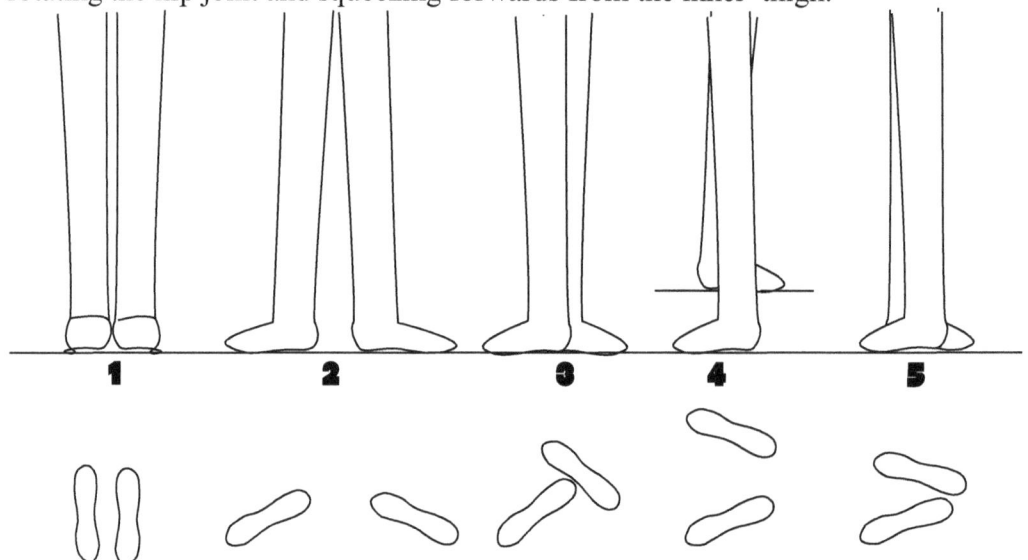

Lesson 2.2 Positioning of Movements

The second element providing consistent stylization in the EDA format of Middle Eastern dance is the positioning of various movements in the body. Each combination of successive movement patterns may be placed at any of these positions - opening up uncountable possibilities for how to express the wonderful expression of Middle Eastern dance.

The illustration gives a defined position for each count in a movement.

The larger numbers signify the main count in movements. For more refined and detailed stylization, the smaller numbers may be utilized to express the technique at it's best.

The concept illustrated may be adapted as shown (front to back) or one may replace the direction indications with top and bottom.

As theory has its limits, here is a practical exercise:

Exercise
Stand with your body aligned front to back, the main count 1 being ahead of you and the main count 3 being behind you.
First place your right leg along the counts in the illustration starting at the small count 1 and continuing clockwise. Continue by placing your left leg along the counts in the illustration.

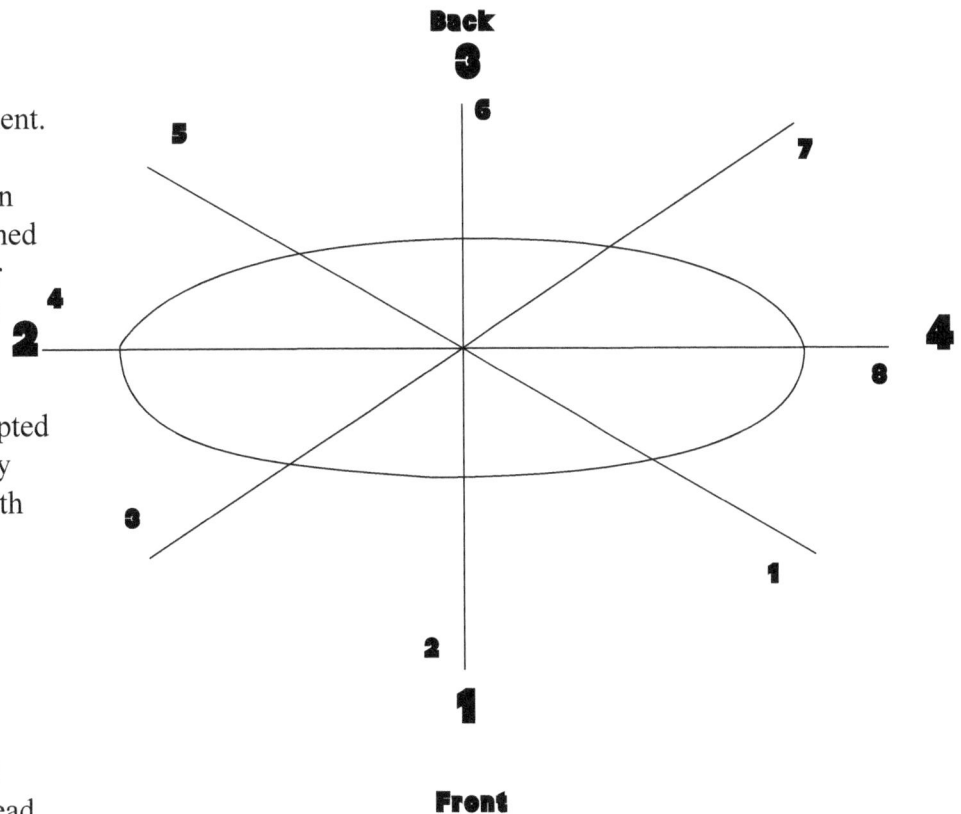

Lesson 2.3 Generating Movements

In today's fitness focused and time constrained society improving stamina, flexibility, strength and saving time are some of the essential qualities we look for in our daily routine as dancers. The EDA bases it's movement philosophy upon muscular movement - in layman's terms that means that all movements are generated by muscles and not by joints or bones. This improves muscle quality, strength and stamina along with flexibility - all preventing injuries and enabling a dancer's career to last longer. Continuous conditioning and working towards understanding the next level of depth to the technique improves the dancer's quality of movement along with awareness of the style and execution of it.

Lesson 2.4   Characters of Movements

Going with the concept of every movement has a meaning or a character, the EDA bases it's philosophy of embedding character into the movements themselves. Combined with expression, emphasis and intention in the movements and facial expressions this gives a complete all encompassing impression of the piece in question to the viewer.

Lesson 2.5   Categories of Movements

The EDA divides movements into the following two categories:
1. accented / emphasized
2. undulating / flowing

Within these two categories there are subcategories such as:
- stationary movements
- traveling movements
- traditional movements
- contemporary movements
- Ballet based movements
- turns

Lesson 2.6   The Significance of Transitions

Many dancers are excellent at executing given movements, however, their weakness in awareness of stylistic expression surface in their transitions. The significance of transitions between movements can not be brought forth enough. Perfection in transitions works as the glue between movements giving a complete and consistent expression in a piece. Further more, stylized and structured transitions ensure consistency and synchronization in movements both in soloists as well as group performances. The EDA divides transitions into the following categories:
1. passing (PS)   - where one body part passes another
2. crossing (X)   - where one body part crosses the path of another
3. redirecting (redir) - where a body part executes a movement redirecting the direction of the body
4. continuing (cont)   - where a body part continues on to the next position

Lesson 2.7   The Music

The Middle Eastern music structure differs from western music. While western music scales are based on tones and half tones Middle Eastern music uses tones, half tones and quarter tones. This system of tones is called Maqamat (plural of maqam) and differs from the western scales with differences more significant to a musician than a dancer. What is significant to a dancer is that these additional tones in the Middle Eastern scaling system and their characters the various maqamat create different moods in their sound - comparable to the terms major and minor in western music philosophy. These tones also makes the sound image of

Middle Eastern music more impacting and fuller, and an untrained ear may miss many of the fine tuned variations in the sounds. The Middle Eastern music structure consists of percussive, wind and string instruments. The most common instruments being;

Percussive		String		Wind	
darabukkah	(drum)	oud	(lute)	nay	(flute)
riqq	(tambourine)	buzuq	(buzuki)	shabbabah	(open-ended, end-blown reed flute)
zagat	(finger cymbals)	kamanjah	(violin)	sournaay/mizmar	(flute)
duff	(larger tambourine)	rabaabah	(2 string fiddle)	mijwiz	(double clarinet)
mazhar	(frame drum)	qanoun	(zither)	argoul	
bandir	(frame drum)	santour	(dulcimer)	qibrah	(bagpipe)
naqqaaraat	(kettle drum)			bouq	(horn)
				nafir	(trumpet)

Additional western and/or electronic instruments such as keyboard, drum set and electric guitar have been added to the repertoire as Middle Eastern has been westernized. Remixed sampling also occurs more and more often as it is a cost effective way of music production compared to the traditional full orchestras.

Lesson 2.8   Artistic Expression and Entertainment Aspect of Middle Eastern Dance

The artistic expression and entertainment aspect of Middle Eastern is strong, emotional, engaging and mesmerizing with strong technical presence and communication with the audience. The technical intricacy of Middle Eastern music and dance allows the dancer to express the music, technique and emotions on various levels simultaneously and successively. Any dancer claiming authenticy within Middle Eastern dance should be expected to express the depth of the technique as well as defend the entertainment aspect of the dance style. The dancer is not only expected to be well educated and well familiarized with both music and technique, but is also expected to present as a true performer in the quality of an actor and dramatize the music, lyrics and situation of the performance on stage.

Chapter 3   Before we start

Lesson 3.1   Finding an instructor

As a student of Middle Eastern dance the first rule is to find an instructor that answers to your needs. Whether you are studying the dance for fun and exercise or to make it your career, the choice of instructor can be detrimental to your progress in achieving your goals if the choice is improper. Make sure that the instructor you choose to study under is someone you respect, someone who's well educated within the dance form and has the focus you seek in their classes. There are countless categories of instructors out there and it is important that your instructor fits your needs. The EDA provides a focused environment with attentive instructors and go-getter attitude. The instructors coach and motivate the students to pursue higher goals and achieve them through dedicated work and disciplined approach.

Lesson 3.2   What to Wear and the Essentials

What you wear to practice is essential to how well your instructor can guide you and provide you with corrective comments. The visibility of the angles of joints, definition of muscles and general proportions is detrimental to the instructor's ability to catch any potential mistakes, and to prevent injuries in a dancer's body. With this as a base, it is a given that wide pants, skirts, t-shirts or even dance costumes are inappropriate in class. Workout wear in stretchy material and fitted clothes such as tank tops, jazz pants, fitted t-shirts etc are recommended. Also, due to all the work on the ball of your foot, it is a good idea to wear *Adult Padded Dance Paws®* in class to protect your feet. Shoes with heels are only recommended if you are working on a piece where heels are a part of the costuming and you need to get used to the difference in weight alignment in the body when dancing on heels. The EDA furthers the restrictions on attire in class by not allowing coined hip scarves in class due to the distraction they provide to the instructor and the students.

To make it easier for you as a student to know what you need, here is a list;
Jazz pant
Tank top
Adult Padded Dance Paws®
Water bottle
Towel
Wrist sweat band
Non-scented/lightly scented deodorant
Hair clip
Correct support undergarments

As certain props are used in Middle Eastern dance, here is a list of the essentials;
Cane - plastic cane wrapped with gold or silver tape
Silk veil - medium weight
Chiffon veil - medium weight
Zagat - finger cymbals, deeper toned. Any metal

Lesson 3.3   Understanding the Necessity of Drilling and Conditioning

Every dance style is a discipline; therefore it should not be necessary to emphasize the necessity of drilling and conditioning. However, since students approach the dance with different motivation it is beneficial to understand why drilling and conditioning is such a weighted aspect of the dance at the EDA.

The worst thing that can happen to dancers' progression in dance is an injury that disables them from continuing to refine their ability and lose valuable time in their development. Considering this and the fact that most injuries happen from lack of strength, failure to maintain posture, lack of body awareness, or just plain old bad instruction the reasoning for why drilling and conditioning is so important is pretty simple;
The more you continue to execute a movement, a sequence or an exercise - the more you increase your strength, body awareness, ability to maintain posture and decrease the potential of injuries. Repetition refines the awareness in execution of a movement and fine tunes the visual outcome. After all, dance is a visual art form and has to look good in order to be perceived as "a beautiful embodiment of the concept of movement".

To make the necessity of drilling and conditioning even more prevalent, here are a couple of examples from other disciplines to compare with;

Every year thousands of children attend Ballet classes all over the world. They undergo continuous strict and stylized training with no room for "personal expression". They have to learn French names for the movements and concepts of movements and do strenuous exercises at the barre. The instructors may demonstrate and explain the movements, but will soon call out the movements and expect them to execute them perfectly. If they do not, they know there will be disciplinary consequences. They have annual examinations. Several will fail. Some of these children will continue on to auditions at Ballet academies in their early teens where a slight Scoliosis, lack of turn out or lack of perfection in the stylization will disqualify them from attending the academy. The ones that are accepted may be disqualified as puberty hits and their bodies change. The remaining few that pass the final exam may never even dream of a soloist spot on a Ballet stage. At auditions they will be surpassed by someone that has a 1 degree better turnout than them or someone will cut up their Tutu in the dressing room while they are visiting the ladies room just because... The minority percentage that make it to those prestigious soloist positions in a Ballet company still get up every morning and stand by the barre doing the same exercises they have been doing since they were 4 years old. Since they will undergo knee, ankle and foot surgeries due to the strain they have put on their body through the years of training.

Millions of children attend Classical Indian dance classes as soon as they learn to stumble around and walk. The instructors give a short demonstration and expect the children to copy it perfectly. Detention is to be expected unless the movements are copied as demonstrated. Explanations are for wimps. These children will continue this rigorous training till they hit puberty. Then their parents may find it inappropriate for a girl or boy "of age" to waste their time on dancing when they should focus on their studies and pass their finals in school. The ones that continue to dance will keep on studying - and quite a few will drop out due to marriage or work. The remaining dancers may graduate their Guru's program in their late 20's or even 30's and then have to stand up against the social dismissal of the artist profession. Further they will be critiqued for their presentation of the 1000 to 4000 year old traditions of Classical Indian dances on each step they take.

Cheerleading - a sport turned into an art form. A teen girl's biggest dream - to shake those pompoms in the air and cheer for their team. Years of practice, tears, sweat and dedication - so brutally crushed at auditions when they don't make into the college cheerleading squad because a certain look, a certain feel and a certain level is expected.

Now what makes those children keep on putting themselves through the agony of rehearsals and practice and continuous harassment from their instructors and peers? What makes parents put their children through it? The same reason for why people do Middle Eastern dances - it is fun and they want to learn it. However, few realize the level of expertise expected of a Middle Eastern dancer - mainly because it is so easy to get a gig at a local restaurant or at your friends' parties. However, this does not dismiss the necessity of quality of dance in the discipline of Middle Eastern dance. Yes, it is a discipline and continuous studies, drilling, conditioning, frustration and achievements are ahead of anyone that wishes to achieve recognition for their work within the field. Any name you will find mentioned in this handbook is a witness of this; they have all stood on the dance floors of numerous dance studios working up a sweat to achieve their goals and the ability to respectfully represent the art form of Middle Eastern dance. And just like in Ballet and Classical Indian dances or even Cheerleading - the student next to them...didn't make it. But, they too had great fun trying their best and celebrating their achievements on the way.

Realizing that no matter what level you are on your body is still your tool and it needs to be conditioned in order to execute the material you give it. It's like a car gets taken in for an adjustment, service and a tune up every X amount of miles to maintain its durability. The same way, a dancer goes to the dance studio to adjust and tune up their technique, refine their movements and maintain the durability of their body.

Lesson 3.4 Complimentary Exercise

After the previous lesson, even the thought of more exercise probably is not very appealing. However, dancers can assist their body's strength and awareness through several complimentary forms of exercise;

- classes in Ballet, Jazz, Flamenco, Modern, Hip Hop, Break Dance, Street dance, Funk, Ballroom, Latin
- gym workouts with focus on core, flexibility and strength
- any form of resistance training
- Pilates, Yoga, Tai Chi
- Kick Boxing, Thai Boxing
- Martial Arts
- gymnastics, aerobics
- biking, swimming, surfing
- skiing, downhill skiing
- snowboarding
...just to mention a few.

Lesson 3.5 Warming Up the Body

Warm ups are the primary way of preventing injuries, without proper warm ups the body may experience the movements as a shocking experience and counter react by contracting the muscles causing tears and sprains. Proper warm ups for Middle Eastern dance should encompass stretches and exercises addressing the neck, shoulders, back, abdomen, arms, hip flexors, hamstrings, inner thigh, calves, ankles and wrists. Further it is important to get proper blood flow going through the body through some light cardio. Movements utilized may be lighter versions of dance movements and flexibility stretches.

Chapter 4   Basic Stylization Exercises

Lesson 4.1   Identifying Placement of Movement in the Body

Taking base in *Lessons 1.1 and 2.2 Positioning of Movements* here is an illustration showing generally what body parts control what type of movements according to the stylization of the EDA.

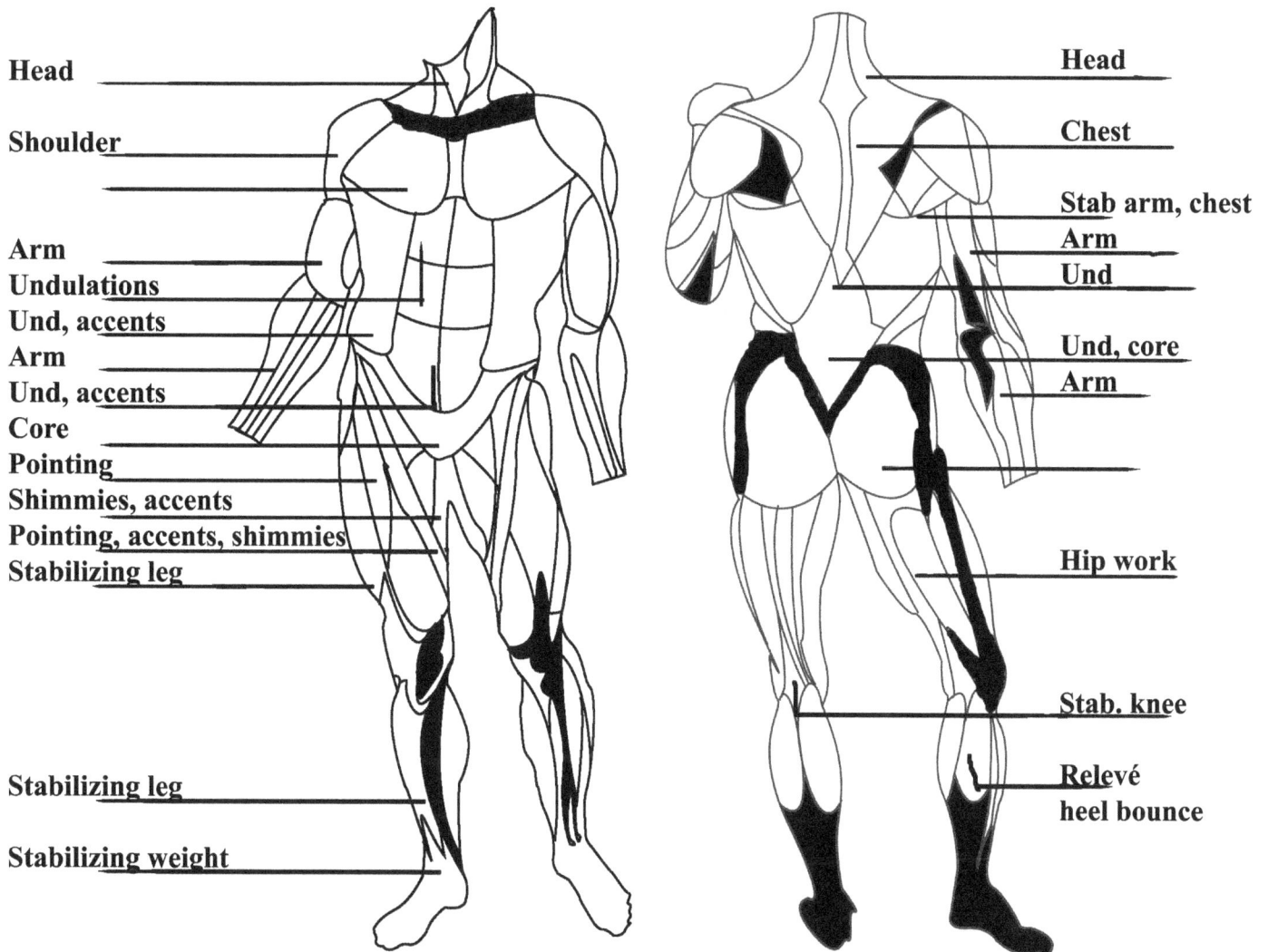

Head

Shoulder

Arm
Undulations
Und, accents
Arm
Und, accents
Core
Pointing
Shimmies, accents
Pointing, accents, shimmies
Stabilizing leg

Stabilizing leg

Stabilizing weight

Head

Chest

Stab arm, chest
Arm
Und

Und, core
Arm

Hip work

Stab. knee

Relevé
heel bounce

Lesson 4.2   The Feet and Legs

Basic exercises conducive to strengthen and stabilize the feet are calf-killers (raise into demi-point and bounce while remaining in demi-point), the ice skater, squats and leg extensions either in folklore posture, neutral posture or in relevé - all exercises that normally are included in the warm up part of a class.

Lesson 4.3 Stepping It Up a Notch With Floor Patterns

As stationary basic exercises can tend to become monotonous a combination with floor patterns can save the day. A combination of various placements of the feet along with steps create patterns on the floor and these patterns are referred to as *floor patterns*. Various floor pattern concepts are included in Middle Eastern dance technique. The most relevant ones however are; the *Chassé*, the *Croisé*, the *Pas de Bourrée*, the *Passé*, the *Step Touch*, the *Lunge*, the *SSA* (step step arabesque) and various kinds of turns.

Practice exercise for floor patterns:

2 x Chassé *RL flat 4 PdP	front back front, front back front
2 x Chassé *RL Rel 4 PdP	front back front, front back front
1 x Lunge *R flat	front
1 x back step *L Rel	back
1 x Croisé turn L *L Sp	cross, turn
2 x Chassé backw flat 4 PdP	back front back, back front back
4 x Croisé R *LRLR flat/Rel	cross step, cross step, cross step, cross step
4 x Croisé L *RLRL flat/Rel	cross step, cross step, cross step, cross step
3 x SSA *RLR, A = Rel	step step arabesque, step step arabesque, step step arabesque
1 x Croisé back turn L *L Rel	cross, turn
8 x PdB *RRLR, LLRL flat	front pivot back back, front pivot back back
4 x Step forw RLRL flat	front, front, front, front
8 x quick tiptoe back Rel	back, back, back, back, back, back, back, back

Other relevant concepts of floor patterns are; BBC (Back Ball Change), KBC (Kick Ball Change), the figure 8, the cross, the cake slice, the square, the circle, the triangle, the diagonal, the rectangle, and similar geometric and organic figures.

Lesson 4.4 Arm Patterns

Another highly relevant, but often ignored, part to stylization are arm positions and even more arm patterns. The way dancers move their arms through the air and let the arm visit certain points of reference create a pattern in the air referred to as *arm patterns*. In Middle Eastern dance as taught at the EDA these patterns are often created by transitions between two points of reference, or more academically referred to arm positions. These transitions may be created by letting the arms cross in front of or behind the body prior to transferring into the next arm position, by transitioning the arms between two arm positions following the alignment axis or by creating an intricate pattern in the air between two arm positions.

Practice exercise for arm patterns:

Transition #4 to #3, 7	cross wrists at sternum
Transition #3, 7 to #4	circular motion over the head to R
Transition #4 to #8	follow alignment axis of the arms
Transition #8 to #4 at heart, 6 at cheek	release from #8, cross at sternum, into positions
Transition #4 at heart, 6 at cheek to #4	align directly with #4
Transition #4 to #4	follow alignment axis, flip hands at #8, open to #4

Lesson 4.5 Combining the Feet, Legs and Arms

Now it's starting to get exciting. Try the practice combination below, the arm positions and patterns are listed above the floor patterns for your convenience:

#4	
2 x Chassé *RL flat 4 PdP	front back front, front back front
2 x Chassé *RL Rel 4 PdP	front back front, front back front

Transition #4 to #3, 7	cross wrists at sternum
1 x Lunge *R flat	front

Transition #3, 7 to #4	circular motion over the head to R
1 x back step *L Rel	back

Transition #4 to #8	follow alignment axis of the arms
1 x Croisé turn L *L Sp	cross, turn
2 x Chassé backw flat 4 PdP	back front back, back front back

Transition #8 to #4 at heart, 6 at cheek	release from #8, cross at sternum, into positions
4 x Croisé R *LRLR flat/Rel	cross step, cross step, cross step, cross step
4 x Croisé L *RLRL flat/Rel	cross step, cross step, cross step, cross step

Transition #4 at heart, 6 at cheek to #4	align directly with #4
3 x SSA *RLR, A = Rel	step step arabesque, step step arabesque, step step arabesque
1 x Croisé back turn L *L Rel	cross, turn

Transition #4 to #4	follow alignment axis, flip hands at #8, open to #4
8 x PdB *RRLR, LLRL flat	front pivot back back, front pivot back back
4 x Step forw RLRL flat	front, front, front, front
8 x quick tiptoe back Rel	back, back, back, back, back, back, back, back

The possibilities are countless and the most traditional arm patterns are what EDA students are exposed to in the beginning of their education. Various dancers have designed signature arm and floor patterns as their stylization and these patterns will be recognized anywhere. As students familiarize with profiled personas in the dance - this will become more and more prevalent to them.

Lesson 4.6 Muscular Focus when Dancing

The philosophy of non-skeletal movement is basically to generate all movements from contractions and expansions in the muscles - positive and negative contractions if you may. Within the EDA concepts of movement this is one of the main pillars creating strong and long lasting dancers and technicians with great body awareness. However, the path to achieving such muscular focus will only happen through consistent, determined and disciplined training. The body is a lazy tool, it tends to get rusty fast if the dancer takes too long breaks from dancing at a time. The key to the EDA concepts is to understand the necessity of mastering body control to achieve finer tuned movements and thereby expanding the vocabulary of movement available to use.

Chapter 5   The Concepts of Movements

Lesson 5.1   Figure 8s

The gray fields in the illustrations to the right act as indicators of neutral positioning of a body part in the movement sequence.

Horizontal forward
1. turn to diagonal angle with R side backwards, *R, lean into 1.
2. bring forward by contradicting diagonal angle.
3. align with body alignment while remaining at diagonal angle.
4. align with body alignment - repeat L

Horizontal backward
1. turn to diagonal angle with R side forwards, *R, lean into 1.
2. bring backward by contradicting diagonal angle.
3. align with body alignment while remaining at diagonal angle.
4. align with body alignment - repeat L

Vertical upward
1. lean and release R into diagonal positioning for 1.
2. push and contract to contradict diagonal angle and reach 2.
3. align with body alignment while remaining at diagonal angle.
4. align with body alignment - repeat L

Vertical downward (Maya)
1. push and contract R into diagonal positioning for 1.
2. lean and release R to contradict diagonal angle and reach 2.
3. align with body alignment while remaining at diagonal angle.
4. align with body alignment - repeat L

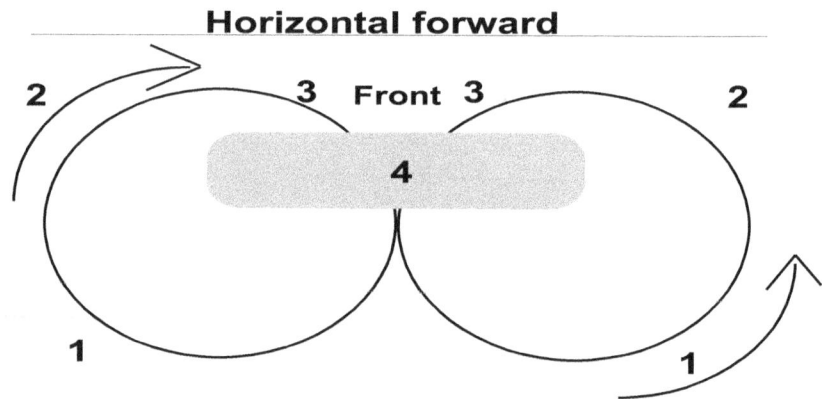

Horizontal forward

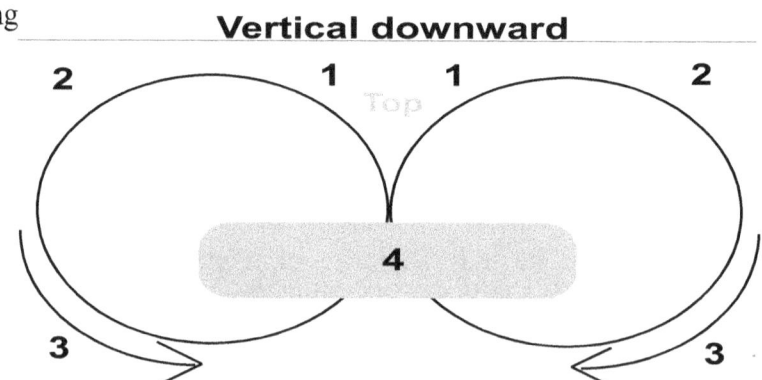

Horizontal bacward

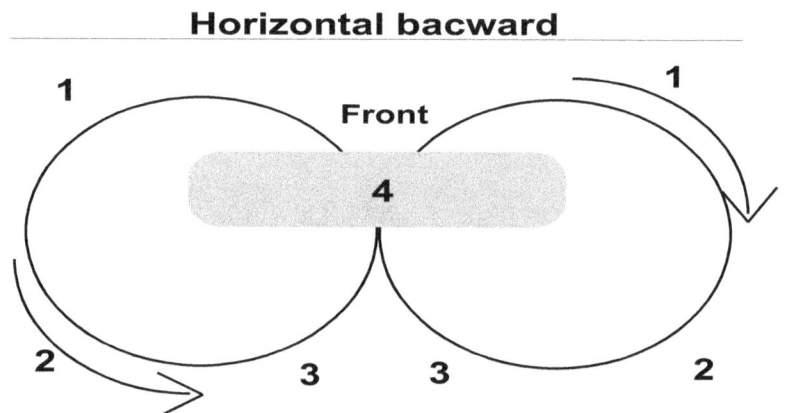

Vertical upward

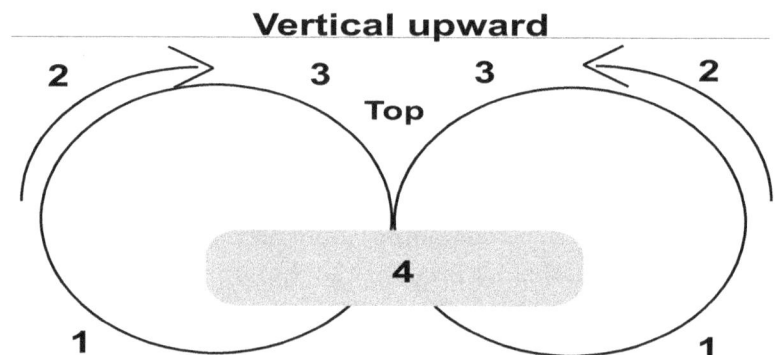

Vertical downward

The figure 8 concepts may be adapted to any body part and are most often used in reference to hip and chest movements. The emphasis on the 3. and 4. count at times is less than 1. and 2. depending on what the dancer finds prevalent in the music as well as a preference choice between folklore and sharki expression of style.

Exciting results occur when different figure 8 concepts are combined in a movement.

Lesson 5.2 Accents

The EDA works by the concepts of muscularly generated movements. Before moving in on the subject of accents it is important to define the 4 states of a muscle according to the EDA movement philosophy:

1. Relaxed
2. Aware
3. Tense
4. Contracted

The technique in this handbook is based upon aware and tense states of the muscles and never releasing into relaxed state nor contracting past the tense state and into contracted state of the muscle.

Accents are created by shortening the time span between the aware state and the tense state of the muscle generating a rapid reaction in the movement. The result of this rapid reaction is called an accent. Accents may be executed with various levels of strength, hesitation and emphasis - resulting in different visual effects. A true dancer will value the effort put into conditioning and strengthening the body to achieve these various levels of strength and body awareness invested in a movement.

A further dimension to an accent can be added through allowing or disallowing the skeleton to follow the contraction movement created when going from aware state to tense state while the muscular contraction is still the primary action. This may create a visual look of extension or contraction of body parts, adding yet another dimension to the visual result a dancer may achieve through accents.

Wrapped up, the EDA operates with the following types of accents:
1. *Static* - muscular contraction, skeleton remains mainly in same position
2. *Dynamic* - muscular contraction, skeleton follows
3. *Extending* - muscular extension of body part
4. *Contacting* - muscular contraction of body part
5. *Redirect* - muscular change of direction
6. *Freeze* - muscular accent with definite stop at return point of movement path
7. *Snap* - muscular accent snapping back from return point of movement path

Typically, accents are created in calves, adductors, hamstrings, quads, obliques, abdomen, rhomboids, lats and triceps.

Lesson 5.3 Undulations

The EDA defines any movement generated by muscular control as a flowing movement unless categorized as an accent as according to the previous lesson. The term used for a flowing movement is *undulation*. Basically, all movements are defined as undulating movements until the time span they are executed within is shortened and they become accents of one or the other kind. Undulations may be combined with accents - giving a different feel and look.

Lesson 5.4 Shimmies

Many confuse the concept of shimmies with the concept of vibrations. In fact, these two concepts couldn't be more different. While shimmies are generated through a relaxed series of repetitive muscular contractions between aware and tense states at various speeds - vibrations are generated by fully contracting the muscles and slightly letting go of the contraction to then return to it repeatedly and rapidly. Whereas shimmies can occur as large slow movement sequences, vibrations are always tight and rapid. Shimmies are present in all 7 types of accents as well as undulating movements.

The most common shimmy is generated from the hamstrings through contracting and releasing between aware and tense states. The look of this shimmy can be impacted by working statically or dynamically, in plié - demi-plié - flat - relevé or by transitioning between various positions and movements while shimmying.

Other shimmies widely used are shoulder shimmies generated by the lats, deltoids and pectorialis/chest muscles.

Theoretically, a dancer can generate a shimmy in any body part by the principle of shimmies as according to the EDA. However, some are not as flattering as others and since dance is a visual art form meant to be esthetic... sometimes it is a good idea not to go there - even if you can go there.

Lesson 5.5 Arms and Arm Patterns

One of the biggest weaknesses seen in Middle Eastern dance, is lack of awareness in arms, positioning of arms and transitions of arms. It is a huge concern as an instructor to see that your students just don't seem to pay attention to the arms. Even worse, the audience's perception of the hard work invested into the dance by each dancer is disvalued by something that so easily can be corrected. To illustrate the significance of arms and arm positions, look at the silhouettes below and see for yourself which one looks more visually pleasant to your own eye.

The EDA principle of arm placement is as follows;
- the shoulder is released onto the lats and the weight of the arm is supported through the lats at all times
    - *even* when the arm is above the shoulder position.
- the arm position is achieved by contracting the triceps and aligning the wrist with the position desired.
- the wrist and middle finger continue the tension and extension of the lats and triceps throughout the arm.
- there is a resistance created against the air as the arm moves through it which enables awareness throughout an arm path and arm pattern.

Lesson 5.6 The Hands

Limp wrists and unawarely placed hands are only yet another witness of lack of body awareness in a dancer and can be detrimental to an otherwise well conditioned and technically disciplined presentation. The EDA therefore works with two basic hand positions; 1) Folklore 2) Raqs Sharki

Folklore hand
The Folklore hand is supported through the wrist and the thumb. The palm gently folds over the thumb and extends the fingers slightly downwards outside the thumb - fingertips aligning with the line created through the wrist and thumb. Fingers remain together, relaxed yet aware, at all times. There is an extension in the middle finger to maintain tension and awareness. The dancer will feel a tension in the flesh between the thumb and the palm as well contradicting the direction of the extension in the middle finger.

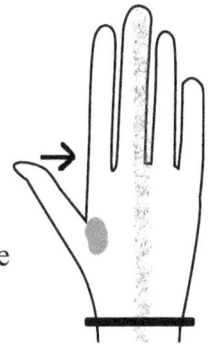

Raqs Sharki hand
The Raqs Sharki hand is based upon the folklore hand. The thumb is placed against the outside of the first joint of the middle finger from the palm. The index finger is extended above the thumb, the ring finger is aligned with the index finger on the opposite side of the middle finger and the pinky extends slightly above the ring finger. There is an extension in the middle finger to maintain tension and awareness. The dancer will feel a tension in the flesh between the thumb and the palm as well contradicting the direction of the extension in the middle finger.

NOTE: do not create a circular shape between the thumb and the index finger as this is a very rude hand gesture in several Middle Eastern and Asian cultures.

There are numerous other hand positions as well that may be incorporated, however, these two are the ones stylized and defined as the two base hand positions of the EDA format of Middle Eastern dance. The main rule for awareness in the hands in Middle Eastern dance is that they are neither static nor dynamic when in position. There is life in the hands - as if the extremities are breathing with the body - unless the dancer decides to chose a static or clearly dynamic expression to increase contrasts in his or her dancing.

Lesson 5.7 DnK - the Drop'n Kick

One of the most widely used and abused movement concepts of Middle Eastern dance is the Drop and Kick - referred to as the DnK (Drop'n Kick) in the EDA terminology. Actually, it should be Drop'n Brush or Drop'n Extend, but since Drop'n Kick is such an incorporated term in the Belly Dance scene, the EDA has incorporated it into the terminology, but emphasize the definition of the movement concept. This versatile concept can be executed in folklore, neutral, relevé, while traveling, stationary, with snap accents, freeze, static, dynamic - the limitations are few!

The DnK according to the EDA is generated as follows:
1. Active hip releases down, the supporting leg generates a snap accent
2. Active hip releases down, the supporting leg generates a snap accent while the active leg brushes the toes against the floor and extends into a point. The obliques contract and pull the pelvic backward distributing the leg evenly on each side of the weight point in the supporting leg.

Lesson 5.8 Stepping Correctly

This brings us to the proper release of the leg and foot from the floor as the return onto the floor. According to the stylization of Egyptian Folklore as per Mahmoud Reda and the Reda Troupe the Ballet based concept of lift and release is also utilized at the EDA. The toes are the last to leave the floor, and the first to arrive onto the floor.

Practice exercise for proper step technique
> Starting in 2nd PdC *L, transfer R in a circular motion to the front while toes are pointed towards the floor ending in 4th PdC. Release R onto the floor - toes, ball of the foot, heel - ending in *R 4 PdP. Repeat L.

Now repeat the following exercise from *Lesson 4.3* slowly while paying attention to the proper step technique.

Practice exercise for floor patterns:

2 x Chassé *RL flat 4 PdP	front back front, front back front
2 x Chassé *RL Rel 4 PdP	front back front, front back front
1 x Lunge *R flat	front
1 x back step *L Rel	back
1 x Croisé turn L *L Sp	cross, turn
2 x Chassé backw flat 4 PdP	back front back, back front back
4 x Croisé R *LRLR flat/Rel	cross step, cross step, cross step, cross step
4 x Croisé L *RLRL flat/Rel	cross step, cross step, cross step, cross step
3 x SSA *RLR, A = Rel	step step arabesque, step step arabesque, step step arabesque
1 x Croisé back turn L *L Rel	cross, turn
8 x PdB *RRLR, LLRL flat	front pivot back back, front pivot back back
4 x Step forw RLRL flat	front, front, front, front
8 x quick tiptoe back Rel	back, back, back, back, back, back, back, back

Lesson 5.9 Level Changes

Level changes are a tool that enables the dancers to change the distance of their body proportions in relation to the floor - sometimes decreasing the distance, sometimes increasing the distance.

Lesson 5.10 Wahed Wa Nous

The movement concept of Wahed Wa Nous (WWN) is widely utilized in the Middle Eastern dance technique and opens up for countless possibilities of layers and movement combinations.

Basically, the Arabic name means *one and a half* and refers to the number of steps the dancer takes in each sequence of this movement concept. The one is a full step and acts as an initiator for the next part. The half is a touch of the ball of the foot to create resistance against the floor and acts as the executor of whatever movement the dancer chooses to incorporate.

In the EDA terminology, the one is most often referred to as the constant and the half is referred to as the variable. This is because the half often is switched out with different movements to achieve a different and exciting expression of the WWN concept. The variable may be a sharp accent, an undulation or a gesture - only the imagination and creative mind sets the limit.

Lesson 5.11 Combining Shimmies and Accents - Samia

This movement concept was named after the legendary *Golden Era* dancer and actress *Samia Gamal* and made famous through numerous movies. The concept is based on the following;
1. a weight transfer onto the active leg in the direction of movement with an accent on the opposite hip
2. continue a shimmy while the opposite leg is placed next to the active leg and the hip is aligned to neutral

This movement concept was traditionally done facing forwards while traveling sideways giving an illusion of the hip dropping below the waist line alignment to then recover. However, as times progress this concept has become one of the more universal movement concepts and can be moved not only in various directions and reversed in order, but also into various body parts - not only the hip.

Lesson 5.12 Jewel of the Nile

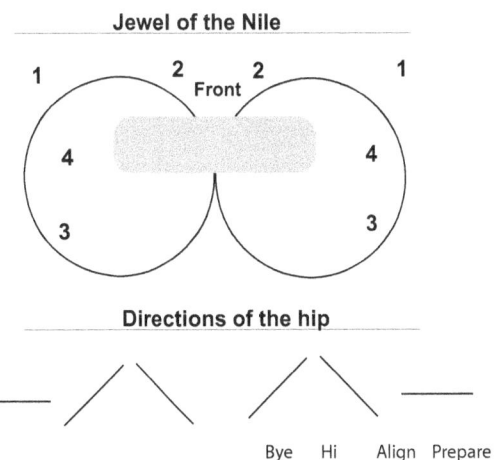

Jewel of the Nile

Directions of the hip

Bye Hi Align Prepare

The *Jewel of the Nile* appears to be one of the more difficult movement concepts to explain as well as learn. Nevertheless, this is how the EDA approaches the Jewel of the Nile.

Jewel of the Nile
1. step onto and transfer the weight to the active leg in the direction of the movement sequence facing diagonal into the direction of origin. The torso remains frontal and level is maintained.
2. the weight remains on the active leg while pivoting in to the direction of arrival and the opposite leg is placed next to it. The torso remains frontal and level is maintained.
3. the pelvic aligns with the torso and the oblique on the same side as the direction of origin is contracted to tense state creating an accent surpassing the alignment of the torso. The torso remains frontal and level is maintained.

4. the oblique is released and the movement sequence is repeated in the opposite direction. The torso remains frontal and level is maintained.

These are the basics of the *Jewel of the Nile*, however, being one of the most versatile movement concepts in Middle Eastern dance - each count can be replaced or layered with other movements making this a quite complicated concept to grasp.

Lesson 5.13 Step Step Arabesque (SSA)

Another eternally adaptable movement concept is the *Step Step Arabesque (SSA)*. Based on the parameters below, this concept allows the dancer to really express their own stylization, expression and creativity to the fullest.

Step Step Arabesque (SSA)
1. step
2. step, prepare arms
3. step - pivot, arms balance
4. prepare for next sequence

Lesson 5.14 Cross Steps (Croisé)

The *Cross Step (Croisé)* is a very versatile movement concept. It allows the dancer to travel far distances quickly with at times intricate foot work. Some instructors refer to combinations of cross steps as "grapevine", but for consistency is has been called Cross Step or Croisé in the EDA terminology. The Croisé opens for intricate transions, rapid placement changes, vigorous and energetic movement patterns and, depending on the combination of Croisé steps, allow even larger parts of the audience to engage in the 3D image of the dancer.

Lesson 5.15 Turns

The turns allow the dancer to be dynamic and energetic on the dance floor just like the Croisé or Cross Steps. There are various types of turns that are included in the EDA vocabulary of a Middle Eastern dancer and here are the most common ones:

Bolero / Boule
The Bolero consists of 1/2 turns or 180 degree turns on each count while stepping in the direction of movement on each turn creating a straight line from point A to point B. The feet are in 1 PdP on each step.

Pivot / Pirouette (P)
The Pivot or Pirouette consists of 2 counts. On the first count the supporting leg pushes off the floor and transfers the weight onto the active leg. The force of the push turns the body around with the active leg as the center and pivoting. On the second count the body returns to default position and the weight transfers back to the supporting leg.

Cross Pivot

The Cross Pivot refers to the fact that the dancers legs/feet cross prior to executing the turn. There are various weight distribution concepts and concepts of crossing and pivoting in this type of turns. A great alternative.

Vueltas Quebradas / Barrel Turns

The Vueltas Quebradas or Barrel Turns are common in Flamenco and Classical Indian dance and refers to the above head arm position the dancer traditionally keeps while executing a Bolero turn in place along with a torso / back bend. It gives the illusion that the dancer's upper body and arms are "stuck" in a barrel while the dancer turns. Thereof the name Barrel turns.

Paddle turn / Sufi / Tanoura turn

The Paddle turn or Sufi/Tanoura turn refers to the way Sufi dancers (eg. Whirling Dervishes and Tanoura dancers) keep their weight focused on one leg while "paddling" around the leg with the other leg.

Lesson 5.16 Jumps and Releases

Jumps and releases display athleticism in the dance along with adding extra emphasis to the dancer's material. They can be utilized as additional emphasis in accents, as transitions, as separate movements or as a gesture. Typically jumps are widely used in stylized folklore (Mahmoud Reda), while releases are typically used in complex Raqs Sharki choreographies - an example being Oum Kalthoum pieces.

Lesson 5.17 Pas de Bourrée

The Pas de Bourrée actually refers to concept from the Bourrée, a dance of French origin common in Auvergne and Biscay in Spain in the 17th century. The French folk dance, with many varieties, is characteristically danced with quick, skipping steps and this is the concept that Pas de Bourrée refers to.

Chapter 6   Layering Movements

Lesson 6.1   The Basic Principles of Layering

The EDA's basic principle of layering is to prioritize the layers according to the audiological image of the music. What is perceived as more prevalent in the music should also be more prevalent in the layer combination either through size, speed, emphasis, visibility, direction or angle.

The key to layering is to completely automize each movement separately, and then synchronize the counts in the movement sequences to achieve the desired outcome. Most students have trouble layering and tend to shy away from layering. This is however one of the key features in Middle Eastern dance and has to be addressed and somewhat mastered in order to claim anything else than knowledge of basic Middle Eastern technique.

The most common problem with layering is that dancers give up too soon. Layering is not easy and requires numerous focused attempts and all of a sudden - it all works! Disciplined and structured repeatetive training is the only way.

The second problem that occurs is that the movements become so small when put together because the dancers are focusing too much on being able to do the layers together at all. However, this is only the first step to becoming comfortable with layering. First thing is to put things together - slow and easy - and relax into the complexity of the layers. The next thing is to practice strength and size in the layers.

The rule of thumb is *strength VS size VS speed*.

Lesson 6.2   Shimmy through it!

One of the things that seem to give great results when it comes to engaging in the wonderful concept of layers is to combine a slow, strong, big shimmy with any movement. Execute the movement slowly while focusing on maintaining the size and strength in the slow big shimmy. Then change the focus from the shimmy to the movement layered onto the shimmy. Once the dancer achieves the desired look and feel - it should be drilled until it just flows naturally in the body.

Lesson 6.3   Contradicting Directions

The beauty of the complexity of layering is that the dancer can combine isolated movements that have movement patterns contradicting each other and achieve interesting and exciting visual outcome - like the following examples:
1. shimmy, ummi CCW, undulation, chest circle CCW
2. hip accents, undulation, chest lift, shoulder shimmy

1. Below 2. Right

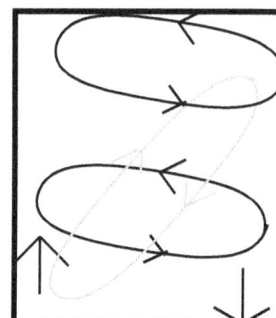

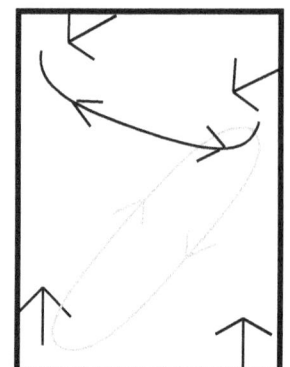

Lesson 6.4 Being Creative

Creativity within a dance style that has a cultural base and presumably several thousands of years of history has a constriction upon the expression of creative combinations and movements; - the feeling, intent, execution and expression of movements have to be maintained to blend in with the cultural expression - not only with the dance technical expression.

This is not only valid within the same dance style, but is also a very significant point when it comes to the concept of fusion; a subject that will be more closely addressed in Chapter 12.

Chapter 7   The Beauty of
Choreography

Lesson 7.1   Remembering it ?!

The beauty and ugliness of choreography really surface when dancers with lack of conditioning, body aware-ness, muscle memory and strength present someone else's works. Misunderstanding of concepts, intention in movements happen and not to forget - the horrific issue of memory.....

The EDA's philosophy around choreographies entails the following aspects:
1. Cultural representation
2. Technical finesse
3. Artistic ability
4. Musicality
5. Seamless transitions
6. Consistent stylization

The only way such a strict and discipline demanding philosophy can be enforced is through also having a clear concept in regard to the approach to choreographies as well - leading to the subject of sequences.

Lesson 7.2   Sequences / Combinations

The EDA's approach to choreography is, as given, through consistently stylized technique. This technique is then put into sequences or combinations to enforce the transitions between the movements and perfecting the musical aspect of the technique such as timing, speed and intent. Sequences are then put into groups / parts / sections and provide seamless transitions in each section - letting the dancer get comfortable in each separate section. By always starting at a set point in the piece, be it the beginning or a clear division between sections, a consistency is created through repetition. The sections are finally put into a full choreography and the dancers are at the end of a work cycle able to execute the given material with confidence, pride and consistency as according to the EDA's philosophy around choreographed work.

Lesson 7.3   Learning Choreographies

Why choreography, you may ask. As brought up at often times in the EDA teachings, consistency is the key to many aspects of the dance - injury prevention, proper technique, stylization, good expression and more. Learning choreography is not an easy task and provides challenging and frustrating moments. However, learning to express someone else's vision, musicality and intention enforces the dancers' ability to associate with the music and to work past any limitations that may be present in them.

Lesson 7.4 Making Your Own Choreography

So, once a dancer learns to express themselves in someone else's vision, then what? Well, then it is time to leap into the exciting chore of choreographing their own material. There are some ideas of how to make even the hardest piece more comfortable to work with.

Find a piece that appeals to you
Consider the fact that you will most probably listen to the piece you work with between 100 - 500 times by the time you put it on stage. It is a good idea to find a piece you really like - and then stick with your decision.

Defining the piece
Defining your piece is an essential part of your vision to the piece. What style of music is the piece? What mood does it call for? Do you envision certain costuming?

Block out the sections
Block out the sections on a piece of paper and give the sections work titles. Use the same work titles for identical sections in the music. I.e. verse 1, verse 2, instrumental 1, chorus etc. This will give you a good framework to work with once you start placing the movements you "hear" in the music.

Identify potential problems
Listen to the piece a few times - pay attention to the rhythms, the rhythm changes, the instrumental changes, the melody line etc in each section. Ask yourself the following questions as you listen:
- What rhythms are present in the piece?
- Are there rhythms you are unfamiliar with?
- Are there sudden rhythm changes?
- Are there abnormalities in any of the rhythms in the piece?
- Do the instrumental changes present any challenges?
- Does the melody line end at the end of the rhythm patterns, or does it continue past the last beat?
- Are there any sounds you want to emphasize especially?

Dance the piece
Dance the piece several times with a video camera on. Don't worry about what it looks like, just jam around and let whatever comes out come out of you. Now review the video and note down what movements you like in each sequence that you did. Now you have a "brainstormed database" of movement suggestions for each section from your own vocabulary.

Listen to and structure out each section
Let the fun begin! Time to start structuring out each section as you listen to it. Don't let the music go past the sequence you are currently working on - it will just make you forget what you just did and move on to the next part before you even had a chance to note things down. Take successive notes of what you come up with. Pay attention to floor patterns, arm patterns, arm placements, body placement, movements, variation in presented vocabulary, repetitions etc.

Walk through it
Walk through your choreography notes in your hands without the music. Don't worry if the pace is slower than intended; just get a feel of how the movements feel in your body. Are there any "funky" transitions? Are there too many repetitions? Is there anything you can change? Make your changes to your notes.

Borrowing from others

There is nothing wrong with getting inspired by other dancers and borrowing movements, combinations or even sequences from them. Giving credits for the material you borrow is a respectful thing to do. However, it is plagiarism to copy someone's material from A to Z, and it is illegal - not to mention that it is just plain rude.

Read and listen

Now listen through the piece while reading the choreography notes, make sure that counts are correct and that what you hear in the music is what you read in your notes. Have you missed any sounds that you would like to emphasize? Have you heard something earlier that isn't in the music or isn't prevalent enough?

Refine the choreography and drill

Make the last changes you want and drill the choreography to perfection.

Stylize the expression

Now start adding expression and costuming details as you rehearse your piece.

If you are new at making choreographies, it is a good idea to lean on your network to help you out. Ask your instructors or dance friends, even non-dance friends, to review the material with you and make suggestions. Are there any changes they suggest? Is there something they really liked that you could bring forth even more?

Lesson 7.5   Getting Inspired

Inspiration is what motivates us dancers to work with a piece or keep on working on our dancing. Getting inspired and actively seeking sources of inspiration is essential to avoid stagnation and boredom. Collect video material of your favorite dancers and performers, compile and organize your class notes, take workshops from other instructors, go see a movie, attend a wedding - anything, really anything, can inspire you to visualizing movement or expression and help you in your work with a piece. If nothing else prevails, ask your friends to help you out.

Lesson 7.6   Giving Creds

One too many times have people made comments such as "oh, that was nothing, I could have come up with that" or "you call that dancing, I could have done it so much better". Well, they didn't, and therefore it is necessary to look into the aspect of recognizing someone else's ability, talent and creativity. Be it a movement, a combination, a sequence or a full on choreography, even a show; dancers and choreographers all have work hard to achieve the level in the material presented and therefore should be accredited accordingly. It is a witness of not being self-absorbed and having a strong character to accredit your sources of inspiration.

Then of course is the issue of workshops or videos. You go out, pay money for the material - you own it, right? No, you only own the right to learn the material, not to claim it as your own. In a perfect world all performances should have introductions such as "XX dancer will present XX piece, originally choreographed by XX, modified by XX and adapted by XX" and "XX dancer will present XX piece inspired by the original works by XX choreographer". There is a fine line between how detailed a dancer and/or instructor should be in their accreditations, but remembering at least where trademark concepts, stylization of movements and combinations came from and giving creds for those is the least minimum expected.

Chapter 8   *Improvisation*

Lesson 8.1 Busting a Move

While choreography is a great way of learning to combine technique and movements into a system expressing a piece of music, improvisation enhances the dancers' ability to respond impulsively to the music which along with consistent training can become a great way of expressing the music. Improvisational dancing brings a different dimension to the dancers' repertoire and allows the dancers to really display their abilities, not only through movement, but also through their level of spontaneous musicality and initial respond time to the music.

Many dancers depend on pre-structured sequences when performing and these structures becomes a safety net for them. However, when improvising - the dancers are allowed to let the music trigger certain sequences of movements in their mind and body without being pre-structured. Their ability to adapt their learned material and respond quickly to any differences in the music is at display along with their technical skill level - an aspect that discourages many dancers from improvisational dancing and refining this tool in their vocabulary.

Lesson 8.2 Daring to Experiment

Improvisational dancing is mostly about courage. Courage to maybe not be 100% accurate in addressing the music, courage to break the monotony of a pre-learned sequence of movements to adapt it to the music, courage to let the music conduct your movements rather than the mind, courage to dare to bust a move and enjoy the result, courage to dare to experiment. Gaining the courage to break all the pre-installed auto-responses to music is what improvisation is about. To spontaneously respond to the music and let the initial movement that comes to mind express itself - movements installed into the vocabulary through consistent training and drilling.

Chapter 9   The Hobbyist

Lesson 9.1   Enjoying the Dance

The initial meeting with the dance can be such a beautiful and exciting experience. Just the joy of movement can provide to a person is truly a wonderful thing to see people experience. Allowing the body to move in ways that seem impossible at first, gaining body awareness and control over the body and muscles - it is all really a great experience. People seek the dance as an outlet for their inner self, to discover their body, to take control over their body, for weight loss or for the experience of trying something challenging and fun. As time progresses in the dance the unity in the class and school is yet another thing that for many people becomes important. That first performance, the first costume, the first dance friend, the first performance video, the first student recital, the first compliment - it all is a part of a very important and strong time in a dancer's life.

Lesson 9.2   "but I just wanna dance" - Setting Your Goals

Although having all these beautiful things in life is important, it is also important to awarely set personal goals for the learning process of dance. Some people attend classes for years and never progress. Although being a hobbyist dancer is about all the factors mentioned in the lesson above, it is also about progression and enabling oneself to take on the challenges of the dance and progress. A common comment often made when the class material seems difficult or the instructor seems too nitpicky is "but I just wanna dance". Yes, it is after all just about wanting to dance, however - no one can "just dance" without learning it first. Everyone remembers those days in our teens when we all copied dance moves off of music videos on MTV or went to a class party and copied the moves of the next person because they were a better dancer than us. Today, let the instructor be your MTV.

People come into the dance for various reasons. Be it self esteem issues, physical issues, psychological issues or just the desire to learn - it is important to set personal goals for the learning experience. Whether it is to loose weight, feel better about yourself or to become the next world famous dancer - none of these goals can be achieved without investing proper effort in class and enjoying the pay-off of that work.

Chapter 10   Taking it to the Next Level - The Professional Dancer

Lesson 10.1   Making it a lifestyle

The hobbyist stage in dancers' careers is so wonderful and fun that many choose to remain in that stage. For those that desire that next step onto the next level - a career as a professional dancer might be it. However, many are under the misconceptions that by taking dance classes, printing business cards, getting a website and buying a couple of costumes - you become a professional dancer. Unfortunately, this is not a fact. These things are all a part of the hobbyist stage of a dancer's career. It's still just all fun and excitement.

Being a professional dancer requires dancers to make aware choices on many, many levels. Choices that shape their future, choices that impact people around them; choices that decide if dancing is a lifestyle or not - for them. Be it the choice between going to class every night or not, going to party with friends or sleeping because you have an important show the day after, eating a carrot or a slice of that juicy creamy cheese cake you have in the freezer, making friends with someone you like or involving in an intimate relationship with them, having a child or waiting a couple of more years before having one, getting that really expensive cruise vacation everyone is going on - or covering your dance class bills and getting a new costume. The aware choices that make a professional dancer a professional do not only involve what costume to wear and what music to dance - it is a daily decision and choice. The dance becomes your life partner and you choose to wake up next to it every morning.

The lifestyle of a dancer consists of conscious dedication to conditioning, injury prevention, drilling to improve and maintain consistency, continuous - almost daily - practice and allowing the body to adapt to the hardship of the profession. No one becomes a strong, vibrant, expressive, technically exceptional dancer over night. It requires not only dedication, but also determination, will power and discipline. Be it how conciously rehearsals and practices are attended or how consciously posture is held outside of class or how conciously a diet is followed to maintain the required and desired look for the profession.

Making a lifestyle of the dance is about replacing any habits with dance relevant body language and health consciousness..... in a perfect world, yes. However, as reality hits - it is mostly impossible to be this perfect of a dancer due to the facts of real life. Most dancers have a primary job that is not dance related as the primary source of income. Most dancers have red numbers on their Excel or Quicken sheets for dance. Most dancers have a life outside dance and most dancers can not live solemnly off of the dance. However, these goals are the ideals that dancers are up against to achieve not only perfection in their work, but also to justify their representational role of the profession and art form.

Orit Maftsir

Frida Bissinger

Sahra

Zahra

Lesson 10.2   The Commitment

What is really required of a professional dancer then? Well, the list is extensive and expands as a dancer's career progresses, however - here is a rough outline to relate to:

- rigorous, continous, dedicated, focused training to ensure quality in the art form
- conforming to a diet to achieve and maintain the required and desired look within the profession
- continued education with instructors and choreographers providing further awareness and challenges
- additional exercise forms to preserve an all around fitness level
- strict attention to and awareness around injury prevention
- a health concious lifestyle refraining from, or at least limiting, alchol, tobacco and illegal substances
- exposure to other dance styles to enhance the body awareness within the style oneself is representing
- attendance and representation at dance/art/culture related events and functions locally, nationally and even internationally
- a rigorously professional representation of the profession both publicly and in private
- network with fellow dancers
- learning the ways of the ethnic groups and cultures involved in the dance form(s) one represents
- researching trends within the dance and update dance vocabulary as needed

Lesson 10.3   A Polished Presentation

The public presentation of a professional dancer does not only reflect his or her own recognition and respect of their own profession, but also reflects the general recognition and respect of the profession within the dance style by everyone involved. What dancers wears to work, how he or she carries themselves, how business is conducted and how the quality of the product is upheld all reflects upon the profession as well as the individual dancer. This responsibility rests upon each worker within any branch - but especially in a profession that is all about appearance and presentation. The entertainment business does not only ask - but demands - great detailed awareness to quality in the services provided as well as public appearance.

By paying attention to skin, fitness level, body image, hair, nails, feet, hands, costuming and not to mention what clothes are worn as representational wear can easily make an immense difference to how a dancer is perceived and also how the recognition of their profession is raised and maintained. Keeping a professional image and presentation is vital for each dancer, but also for the profession's recognition in general. A less approached subject, but just as vital is the subject of age and size appropriate costuming as a dancer.

Lesson 10.4   Networking

Just like in other paths of life it is essential to create a network within the dance as well. Dance friends and colleagues provide not only someone to share the dance with and to find support in, but also an important quality control mechanism for a dancer's work.

Another aspect of networking is creating friendships across school, troupe, instructor affiliations and across the map. Long lasting friendships and work relations have bloomed from just a friendly greeting or approach to fellow dancers and others involved in the dance. Networking at events, work places and in class can open unimaginable doors.

Lesson 10.5   Marketing

So lets say you invest all this time and money into dance classes and costumes, make lots of dance friends and attend all kinds of events....but no one knows who you are. Why? Because your marketing is non-existent. In today's world of competition and people being bombarded by impressions and advertisement constantly - it is vital to have good, individual, contemporary, visible and available marketing through websites, ads in print media, business cards and merchandise. Starting at a professional logo and ending at wearing your own name on your clothes - branding creates awareness around your services and existence. Not only is a recognizable brand important, but also a thought out concept of your product. What style(s) do you claim? What do you deliver? What makes you unique? All these questions and more define a dancer's marketing.

Lesson 10.6   Etiquette and Conduct

The business of entertainment focuses not only on talent and appearance, but also on behavior and presentation. As a professional performer the lines between public and private appearance become less defined and the dancer needs to evaluate his or her behavior in all dance related situations carefully, sometimes even situations that aren't dance related. It is not only expected that the dancer is aware of etiquette and conduct in the country they are presently residing in - but also in the countries and cultures they visit. For a Middle Eastern dancer that would entail learning about and emersion into the cultures of the Middle East and the characteristics of the ethnic groups from the Middle East.

First and foremost, a dancer's conduct with his or her peers sets a stage for fellow artists' perception of the dancer and the product available through the dancer. Just being a fabulous dancer is not enough if you are impossible to work with or lack manners. Being approachable and have integrity is a vital trait of the business. Pretending that everything is ok, when things are not, is not going to solve anything neither does acting improperly just out of the blue. A short conversation can be the instant solution to misunderstandings between peers be it in class or out and about in the life as a professional dancer. Dancers are creative people and creativity desires an aware emotional life, so misunderstandings and outbursts are an understandable part of the game. However, letting things go without resolving situations or excusing bad behavior is not the solution. A dancer should therefore pull the colleague in question aside and handle any potential weirdness instead of letting issues prohibit their productivity and coloring off on their behavior. To quote the hilarious comedienne Kathy Griffin from her show *Everybody Can Suck It* on how not to handle things; "I was raised right, I talk about people behind their backs. It's called manners?!"

Another venue etiquette and proper conduct is expected is when relating to potential employers or sponsors. Many dancers have a primary job and have the dance as a secondary job - even as a semi-professional hobby. This does not make it ok to be any less professional with work connections. Each employer and sponsor deserves the respect and recognition for their position in spite of any bad prior experiences or rumors one may have heard. Even if a dancer experiences a bad situation with an employer or sponsor, the dancer is expected to maintain dignity and professional conduct throughout the work relation. If you're not having a good time of it, then fulfill your currently scheduled responsibilities and excuse yourself from future obligations. Less than professional conduct will only reflect badly upon the dancer and their work.

Just as important as peers, employers and sponsors are the fans and audience members. Each audience member makes an honest effort and investment to see a dancer's presentation and they expect the same in return. The investment may just be symbolic - like dressing up and going out for dinner and enjoying an evening out where a dancer appears. However, the investment deserves recognition and respect. A dancer is expected to act cordially and treat all patrons, fans and audience members with equal respect. Therefore it is important to set the ground rules clearly when performing. A dancer with a cheap presentation, bad technique, improper gestures and/or insecure appearance is more likely to have a bad experience at work than a dancer with a good presentation, decent technique and a secure, confident approach. Basically, if your audience member feels that you have prepared yourself and your presentation well - they are more likely to respect you and give you recognition for it as well.

Basically the golden rule of thumb as a professional dancer in relation to others around you is to keep personal emotions out of business and solve any unpleasantness as privately and discretely as possible.

Lesson 10.7　　　The Role of The Professional Dancer

Mainly, there are a few things that define the role of a professional dancer. Primarily, the professional dancer's role is to provide quality entertainment in dance in a professional manner and appropriate for their audiences. Furthermore, a professional dancer has a representational responsibility on behalf of the style(s) he or she dances, his or her peers, his or her profession as well as their own business. Additionally, a dancer is to present the audience with material and expertise not available to the audience "in the comfort of their own living room".

The dancer is also responsible for making the audience feel comfortable and at ease during his or her presentation. This includes appropriate costuming and presentation for age and size. Dancers embody esthetics and beauty to their audiences - most often according to the mainstream perception of these two. Also, in today's society where pedophilia and indecent behavior towards women and children is reported daily on the news - it is important to take these aspects into consideration as well. At the strictest definition of this, the EDA distances itself from children under the age of conscent appearing in too revealing costuming, i.e. exposure of cleavage or chest, thighs, midriffs and/or visible underwear. As for dancers of adult age - similar rules apply in regards to a professional presentation.

Understanding the strong ability to affect the audience is important for every dancer. The dancer has immense power over the audience's experience when on stage and it is an essential part of being a professional dancer to research and take upon oneself the responsibility of the audience's experience.

Lastly, but just as important, the Middle Eastern dancer is expected to present some level of modesty when not on stage. This calls for the equally endeared and detested cover up garment to be an essential part of the Middle Eastern dancer's gig bag.

Chapter 11   The Instructor
- Bringing a Legacy Further

Lesson 11.1   The Representational Responsibility

Being an instructor of Middle Eastern dance entails several responsibilities and among those is the representational responsibility of the dance style(s). Each instructor is a responsible for having an in depth understanding of the style, not only technically but also culturally, in order to do fulfill their representational role to their students as well as their audiences. What does that mean, you may ask yourself. It is very simple, an instructor is not only expected to know about the culture associated with the dance(s) he or she represents, but also to understand it for the role it plays in the society where the dance(s) comes from. Correct cultural representation is essential to avoid misunderstandings and act as not just an ambassador but also as a bridge builder between cultures and societies. It is indeed a great responsibility and should not be set aside due to its vastness.

Lesson 11.2   The Scholastic Aspect

An instructor's responsibility does not only restrict itself to representation and technique, but also encompasses a requirement of a scholastic aspect to their activities including a set curriculum, goals for their students and rewards to mention a few. Be it a beginner class or advanced professional rehearsals for an international performance - the necessity of structuring out the scholastic aspect, which includes the ability to clearly explain the anatomy and desired visual result of a movement, choreography or expression.

Lesson 11.3   The Ethical Burden

Another responsibility resting on the shoulders of an instructor is the ethical burden of providing the students with the necessary information to understand and execute the dance as efficiently and well as possible. This does not only entail coming up with the curriculum for the classes, but also continuing education to continuously enrich and develop one's own rapport actively either through research, self studies and/or through pursuing instruction from other instructors.

Lesson 11.4   Promoting yourself

Although there are great tools of marketing out there such as print material and websites, the best promotion an instructor can do for him or herself is to invest into their students and let their skill level reflect the instructor's ability to teach and encourage growth in their students. The visual result and the personal recommendation from a student or fan have high value to the instructor.

Lesson 11.5   The Role of The Instructor

The role of the instructor is simple, but vast; provide the students with the necessary information, encouragement and motivation to work hard at their dancing and continuously grow within the dance.

Chapter 12   Preserving the Legacy of Egyptian Style

Lesson 12.1   Technique VS Style

As one of the most clearly defined Belly Dance styles, Egyptian Raqs Sharki - and folklore - there is a clear value of preserving this artistic expression. However, not everyone can, or want to, "dance like an Egyptian". Therefore it is important to understand the value various roles play. Most dancers today focus on technical ability and execution. A minority of dancers emphasize on the stylistic expression and feel of the technique. One may discuss the presumed deception of executing the technique without the stylistic expression and feel, however - both groups of dancers are doing an invaluable duty on behalf of the Egyptian Raqs Sharki style.

In a both culturally and artistically understanding environment, it is less noticeable to the viewer if the technique or stylistic expression has been adapted to its surroundings. This adaptation becomes more visible when looking at Egyptian style dancers on other continents and outside the Arab world. Continents such as Europe, Asia, North and South America have significantly pronounced characteristics that differ from the typical Egyptian style of Egypt. Characteristics that most commonly are expressed through the stylistic expression of the dance such as emphasis and hesitation in movements, incorporation of folklore elements and culturally specific gestures often are put aside in an attempt to achieve a more audience friendly and thus less culturally specific expression.

There are pros and cons in putting more emphasis on technique or on style, however there is no easy answer to whether technical excellence replaces the necessity of culturally and stylistically specific elements in order to achieve a proper preservation of the Egyptian style of Raqs Sharki, or if culturally specific and stylistically specific elements play a significantly more important part in the portrayal of the style.

The dancer has to take into consideration the factors of 'user friendly' presentation, venue and audience, and whether the dancer's role is to appear as a cultural ambassador, a novelty act, a part of a variety show or as an artistic/technical representative of the dance style. Whereas some venues ask for a higher level of artistic/technical representation other venues may require a higher culturally representative content. Each dancer has to define their own role in the dance; whether it's been being a cultural ambassador or an artistic/technical representative, both roles play an irreplaceable part as ambassadors for the dance style.

It is necessary to realize that both cultural ambassadors and artistic/technical representatives play an equally important part in conveying the dance style to the general public. Stylistic loyalty is not only defined by being a cookie cutter carbon copy of famous Egyptian performers, but also through the technique utilized in a dancer's material and performances. The definition of an Egyptian style dancer is not only done by the stylistic expression and feel of the technique, but also but what technique and what concepts are used.

Each culture and each country has its own expectations upon professionalism and artistic presentations. Therefore in order to achieve a higher recognition of the dance style dancers may have to adapt the stylistic expression to these expectations in order to achieve a more audience friendly presentation. This merrily establishes a stylistic adaptation of the style and not a new or redefine style - as long as and the majority of the technical parameters and concepts still remain the same.

Lesson 12.2   Western Dance Philosophy VS Eastern Dance Philosophy

The most predominant detriment to a dancer's ability to absorb information from various instructors from different cultures is depending on one form of communication. Yes, it is easier to understand an instructor that continuously dismantles each movement and concept, however, words can only reach so far. The aspects of physical, audiological, and visual perception are essential for a dancer aiming towards a fulfilling understanding for the Middle Eastern dance, or any dances from the Eastern countries. After all, the dancer is the visual embodiment of the music through the visual, physical and emotional presentation and leads the viewer through a visual and emotional journey with his or her presentation.

Is is great to have body awareness enough to understand the verbal explanation given by an instructor, but it is also important to perceive the visual result desired and the quality of movement that differentiates a great technician from an artist.

Lesson 12.3   AmCab, Oriyantal Tanzi, ATS, ATF, Lebanese and Egyptian Raqs Sharki

While avoiding the never-ending discussion of the purity of styles, the quality of styles and the discussion in regard to "rivalry" between styles, the EDA aims to work as a bridge builder between styles. The EDA's philosophy is that different folklore traditions, dance technical influences and basic posturing results in a different appearance in the different styles. Ideally, a dancer of recognized caliber should at the least expose him or herself to other styles - or even aim to justfully represent them as well.

Lesson 12.4   To Fuse or Not to Fuse, That's the Question!

Many performers get turned off by the restrictions of culture and styles imposed upon them through the dance scene and continue on to explore their own expression within the arts. However, as mentioned previously - you can only explore something you know or learn how to do. Bottom line, it means that dancers aiming to present fusion have the responsibility of in-depth studies of each and every style they aim to combine in order to preserve the integrity and quality of the various styles they wish to combine. Sometimes this entails continuous studies within several styles in order to preserve objectivity and justfully pursue the individual artistic expression. A defined and updated understanding of a style only confirms a dancer's ability to create innovative pieces and fusion. Fusion can be a beautiful outlet for creativity and innovation, however, the quality of dance should not suffer when fusing various styles.

Lesson 12.5   Preserving the Quality of Movement

Preserving the quality of movement...oooh, big words and it sounds great. However, reality is that it is probably one of the hardest tasks of a dancer. Slight modifications to the quality of movement can give tremendous results in the outcome of a movement, combination or piece. Realizing the responsibility of preserving the quality of not only presentation and vision, but also movement is vital to a performer looking to grow within any style - especially Egyptian style. The difference is easily defined by looking at the difference between a mere technician and an accomplished artist. Due to the cultural connection of Egyptian style - it is expected that the dancer preserves the cultural quality and significance of a movement as well as the general quality of it. Indeed a comprehensive task well worth taking upon oneself as a dancer.

Lesson 12.6   The Importance of Consistent Conditioning

Everyone that has learned to ride a bike, put it away for a few years and then picked it up again will remember the clumsy feeling when getting back on the bike. It's like the knowledge and ability of riding it is still there but very rusty. The same goes for the knowledge and ability of dance; just because a dancer achieves a high level of knowledge and ability at one point in life does not automatically mean that the fine tuned mechanics of the body remain consistent through a hiatus. This is why the importance of consistent conditioning is not only high, but essential in a dancer's journey.

Lesson 12.7   Staying Updated

After having reflected on lesson 12.6 it is pretty obvious why staying updated is essential to a dancer's career as well. Outdated material can be detrimental to a dancer's presentation and reception by the audience. Consistent training, conditioning, experimenting, pursuit of instruction and growth opportunities should be an aware and conscious focus in each dancer's mind as they go through their career. Especially as the years of dancing and experience start hitting double digits and a lot of things start running on autopilot.

Chapter 13   The Holistic and Therapeutic Aspects of Dance

Lesson 13.1   The Holistic and Therapeutic Aspects of Dance

The EDA does not coin itself as a school with a holistic focus in its curriculum, however we do recognize the holistic value of dance. Dance can be a great way of increasing body awareness and discover physical and emotional aspects to one's body and person. Furthermore, the EDA also recognizes the value of energy flow association in movement without making that our main focus in our teachings.

Dance is a great mode of stress release and changing negative energy to positive energy through increased sense of self empowerment and awareness. Not only that, but dance also can contribute to appreciation for the beauty of the physical, emotional and visual mechanics of the body.

Another aspect often contributed to dance is the use of dance as trauma therapy with patients that have gone through misfortunate experiences or accidents.

Chapter 14   Reference Library

I   *The Names of Relevance - The Egyptians

The Golden Era - the Era of Elegance
Samia Gamaal
Tahia Cariocca
Naima Akef

Pre-Reda - The Era of Old Skool
Fifi Abou
Nagwa Fouad
Lucy
Mona El-Said
Suheir Zaki

Reda Folklore - The Revolution
Mahmoud Reda
Farida Fahmy
Yousry Sharif
Aida Nour
Raqia Hassan
Ahmed Fekry
Mohamed Shahin
Mohamed El-Hosseny

Post-Reda - The Sharki Heritage of Reda
Aida Nour
Raqia Hassan
Dina
Randa Kamel

The Kaoumayya Troupe
Faten Salama
Lubna Emam
Freiz

Other Significant Egyptian Names
Momo Kadous
Magdy El-Leisy
Dandash
Khaled Mahmoud

*list is limited to names whom have directly contributed to the EDA technique and concepts

II   *Egyptian Style Dancers From Other Continents

North America
Zahra Zuhair
Sahra Saeeda
Bahaia
Roxxanne
Jillina
Aisha Ali
Judeen
Lilla Varese
Lucy / Amar
Farhana Masri
Dahlena
Shareen El-Safy
Debbie Smith

South America
Lulu Sabongi
Sorraya

Europe
Lee Figenschow
Hilde Lund
Michelle Galdo
Helene Skaugen
Siw Øksnes
Majken Wærdahl
Tina Rasmussen
Ulrika Hellqvist
Lena Helt
Suzanne Petrén Abou Shebika
Kay Artle
Konstantina Buni
Annika Vallgren
Frida Bissinger
Ulduz Salimian
Kamelia
Horacio Cifuentes
Beata Cifuentes
Samassem
Yasmina
Saida
Nour

*list is limited to names whom have directly contributed to the EDA technique and concepts

III   The EDA Lineage & Pedigree

← **Stephanie Heuer** ←
Jamila Salimpour
Suhaila Salimpour

← **Siw Øksnes** ←
↑
Ulrika Hellqvist
Raqia Hassan
Aida Noor
Sammasem
Beata Cifuentes
Horacio Cifuentes

Houman
Ninna Holdbek
Djamila Henni Chebra
Assia Guemra
Sadia Sohyah
Mari Al Fajr
Sami El Desoki
Farida Fahmy
Shareen El Safy
Morocco

← **Lee Figenschow** ←
↑
Ulrika Hellqvist
Lena Helt
Raqia Hassan
Aida Nour
Randa Kamel
Ahmed Fekry
Samassem
Beata Cifuentes
Horacio Cifuentes

Ninna Holdbek
Kay Artle
Shareen El-Safy
Farida Fahmy
Mukhtar Mustafa
Denice Enan
Morrocco
Djamila Henni Chebra

← **Hilde Lund** ←
↑
Ulrika Hellqvist
Lena Helt
Raqia Hassan
Aida Nour
Randa Kamel
Samassem
Suzanne P. A. Shebika
Mona El Said

Lina Koureh
Shoshanna
Ibrahim Akef
Mahmoud Reda
Nadia Hamdi
Rachida Reguig
Kay Artle
Ninna Holdbek
Morocco
Nourhan Sharif
Djamila Henni Chebra
Mounira Yagobi
Saida Sohayah
Gamila El Masri
Shareen El Safy
Fahd Khayali

← **Ulrika Hellqvist** ← Bahi Barakat

← **Lena Helt** ← Mahmoud Reda
Suheir Zaki
Lubna Emam

↑

Raqia Hassan
Aida Noor
Samassem
Yousry Sharif

← **Zahra Zuhair**

↑

Raqia Hassan

← **Aida Nour** ← Mahmoud Reda
Samia Gamaal
Naima Akef
Taheya Cariocca

← **Raqia Hassan** ← Mahmoud Reda

← **Randa Kamel** ← Mahmoud Reda

↑

Raqia Hassan

← Kay Artle ← Suraya Hilal
Carolina Nericcio

← **Suzanne P.A. Shebika**

↑

Raqia Hassan

← **Konstantina Buni** ← Ibrahim Akef

↑

Lena Helt
Aida Nour
Raqia Hassan

← **Samassem**

← Majken Wærdahl

↑

Raqia Hassan

← **Frida Bissinger**

↑

Raqia Hassan
Aida Nour
Yousry Sharif
Lena Helt
Suzanne P.A. Shebika

← **Annika Vallgren** ← Lubna Emam
Emira
Gassan Kanaan
Cahit Cosar
Munira Al-Enezi
Shiva Shahandeh

↑

Raqia Hassan
Aida Nour
Yousry Sharif
Konstantina Buni
Lena Helt
Suzanne P.A. Shebika
Randa Kamel
Samassem
Suzanne P.A. Shebika
Mohamed A. Shebika

← **Sahra Saeeda** ← Mahmoud Reda
Farida Fahmy

← **Jillina** ← Momo Kadous

↑

Raqia Hassan
Aida Nour
Zahra Zuhair

← Majken Wærdahl

Raqia Hassan
Aida Nour

← Bahaia ← Shakira
Dahlena

↑

Aida Nour

← **Yousry Sharif** ← Mahmoud Reda

← **Ahmed Fekry** ← Mahmoud Reda

← Dina ← Mahmoud Reda
Ibrahim Akef

↑

Raqia Hassan

← **Dandash**

↑

Raqia Hassan
Aida Nour

← Orit Maftsir   ←   Mahmoud Reda
                                   Farida Fahmy
                                   Dina

Raqia Hassan
Aida Nour
Randa Kamel

← Fahtiem   ←   Ibrahim Farrah

Aida Nour
Raqia Hassan

← Patrisha Gutierrez ←   Arlene
                                Judeen
                                Anaheed
Fahtiem   Shareen El-Safy
                                Angelika Nemeth
                                Feiruz Aram
                                Tilana
                                Halame
                                Harry Saroyan
                                Helen Bilazekjian
                                Mike Solakian

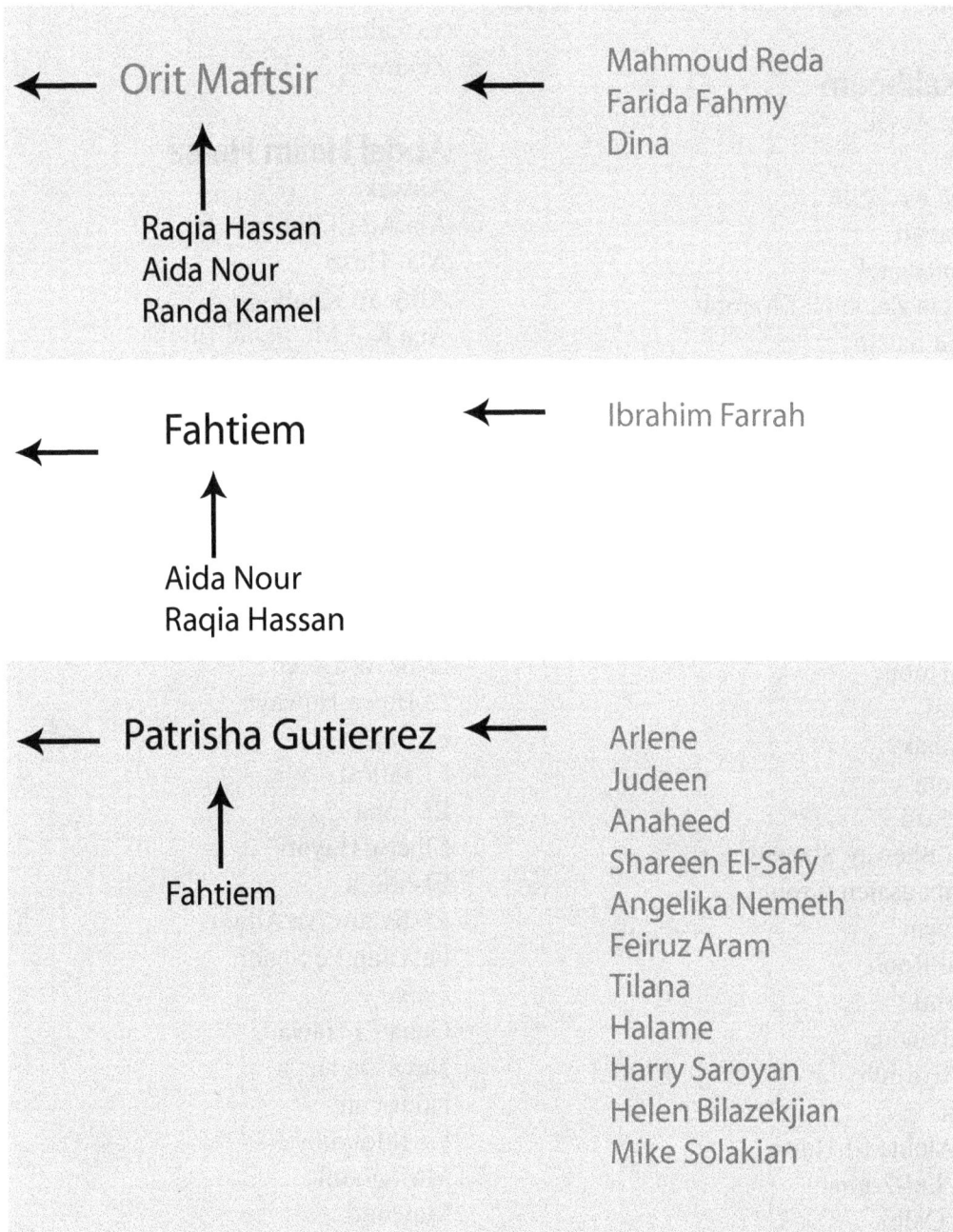

Disclaimer: Information is based on websites and conversations with the mentioned artists. The EDA Lineage & Pedigree is based on the EDA's sources of knowledge and inspiration along with instruction and long time studies.

Instructors in larger black font = names whom have been attended studies with
Instructors in larger gray font = relevant sources of knowledge and inspiration
Instructors in smaller black font = names with cross reference of studies
Instructors in smaller gray font = names with no-cross reference of studies

IIII   Significant Musical Pieces

Oum Kalthoum

Aghadan Alqak
Al-Atlal
Alf Leila we Leila
Amal Hayati
Ana F'entezarak
Ana Wenta Zalamna El-Hobb
Ansak Ya Salam
Aqbal Al-Layl
Arak Asey Al-Damii
Arooh Lemeen
Awwedt Eini
Beeid Annak
Dalili Ehtar
El-Hobb Keda
El-Hobb Kolloh
Enta El-Hobb
Enta Omri
Esaal Rohak
Fakkarooni
Fat El-Maad
Ghannili Sheway Sheway
Ghouloubt asaleh fi rouhi
Ya Karawan
Hadith al Rouh
Ouzkourini
RiHab al hudda
Hadith Al-Rouh
Hagartak
Hakam Aleina El-Hawa
Hasibak Lel-Zaman
Hayyart Qalbi
Hazihi Laylati
Hobb Eih
Howwa Sahih El-Hawa Ghallab
Koll El-Ahebba
Kull laylah wi-kull yum (betfakkar fi min?)
Leilet Hobb
Lel-Sabr Hodood
Lessa Faker
Men Agl Aynayk
Rubaiyat Al-Khayyam
Raq el Habib
Siret El-Hobb
Ţareeq WaHed
Toof we Shoof
W' Daret El-Ayyam

Ya Msaharni
Ya Zalemni
Zekrayat

Abdel Halim Hafez

Ahwak
Ala Ad El Sho'o
Ala -Hezb
Alby Ya Khaly
Ana Kol Ma'agoul Eltoba
Ana Lek Alatool
Ashanek Yaamer
Assmar Ya Assmarany
Awel Marra
Bahlem Biek
Balash Etab
Bea'a Albek
Bokra W'Ba'adou
Dehk W'Le'eb
El Hawa Hawaya
El Layaly
El Talaba
El-Toba
Elhelw Hayaty
Elshou'a
Essba'any Ya Alby
Fe Youn Fe Shahr
Gabar
Gana El Hawa
Heya De Heya
Kont Fen
La Taloumny
Mashghoul
Mawood
Mien Ana
Na'am Ya Habiby Na'am
Nar
O'abalek
Oulolou
Sawah
Shaghalouny
Sodfa
Toba
Ya Alby Ya Khaly
Ya Khalai El Alb
Ya Malek

Farid El-Atrash

Albi Wa Moftaho
Ana We Enta We Bass
Awal Hamsa
Busrat Ir Rih
Eish Anta
Gamil Gamal
Hayah Helwa
Hebbina Hebbina
Hekryat Gharami
Ma Alli Wi-Oltilo
Rabeeh
Wayak
Ya Gamil Ya Gamil
Ya Habibi Ya Ghaybeen
Ya Salam Ala Hobi We Hobak
Ya Zahratan Fi Khayali
Yahliw
Zeina Zeina

Mohamed Abdul Wahab

Ah Minnak Ya Garihni
Al Fan
Al Habib Al Maghoul
Al Kamh
Al Neel
Al Nahr Al Khalid
Al Siba Wal Jamal
Al Qamh
Ahibbo Mahma Ashouf
Ala Bali Ya Nasini
Ala Eh Bitloumni
Albi Bi Oulli Kalam
Ana Elli Toul Omri
Ala Ghosoun El Ban
Ana Antonio
Ana Wil Athaab We Hawak
A'shik Al Rooh
Abeltu Wu Yareyt Ma Abeltu
Ahib Eishet El Hurriya
Ahibbak Winta Fakirni
Ahoun Aleyk
Alashan El Showk
Algondool
Allamuhu Kayfa Yagfu
Amana Ya Leyl
Ashiq El Rouh
Ashki Le Meen El Hawa
Assiba Wal Gamal
Ayyu Sirrin Feek

Aziza
Bafakkar Filli Nassini
Balak Ma'a Meen
Balash Tiboosni
Bileel Ya Roohi
Billah Ya Leil
Bulbul Hayran
Dahheit Gharami
Dijla
Eh Gara Ya Albi
Eh Inkatab Li
El Alb Yama Ntazar
El DhuIm Da Kan Leh
El Dunya Sigara Wu Kas
El Hawan Wayyak Ma' azza
El Kas Beyn Idayya
El Leyl Yetawwil Alayya
El Mayya Terwi El Atshan
El Neel Magashi
El Sabre Wel Iman
Eftekirni
Egri Egri
Elli Enkatab Al Gebeen
Elli Yihebb El Gamaal
Esmah Wu Oulli
Emta El Zaman
Fakarouni
Feyn Tareeqak
Fil Bahr Lam Futtukum
Fil Leyl Lamma Kheli
Gabal Al Towbad
Gafnuhu Allama Al Ghazal
Ha Ullik Eh An Ahwali
Habib El Alb
Habibi Le'beto
Hagrani Leh
Hakeem Oyoun
Halleyt Ya Rabi'
Hamsa Ha'rah
Hananak Bi Ya Rabbi
Hasadouni Wu Bayin Fi Oyounhum
Hin Yalli Hagart El Rouh
Hub El Watan
Icheqt Rohek
Illeel Lama Khili
Indama Ya'ti El Masa'
Insa El Dunya
Inta Inta
Inta Wu Azouli Wu Zamani
Jafnuho Allama Alghazal

Kalat
Kan Agmal Yowm
Karawan Hayran
Keteer Ya Albi
Khai Khai
Khay Habibi Leh Assi
Khayef Aqul
Kilobatra
Kolleda Kan Leh
Kullina Nihib El Amar
Kul Elli Hab Intassaf
La Mush Ana Illi Abki
La Takthibi
Lamma Enta Nawi Tigheeb
Lastu Adri
Layali Ramadan
Leylet el-Wada'
Ma Kanshe Al Bal
Mahla El Habib
Majnoon Layla
Makadeeru Min Jafnayki
Mashghoul Bi Gheyri
Maqadir Min Gafnayki
Mawkib Ennoor
Men Ad Eh Konna Hena Roddi Alayya
Meen Azzibak
Min Zayyik Andi
Miskeen Wu Hali Adam
Mudnaka Gafahu
Nadani Albi Eleiki
Olli Amallak Eih Albi
Ooli Aamallak Eeh Albi
Ougibat Bi
Qasidat Al Khataya
Roddat ElRouh
Sa'it Mabasoofak Ganbi
Saherat Minhu El Layali
Seket Leih Ya Lissani
Set Elhabayib Ya Habiba
Shabakouni Wu Nisyouni
Tal Intizari
Talaffatat Dhabiyat Al Wadi
Tera'eeni Qirat
Toul Omri
Walla Mana Sali
Ya Dil Na'eem
Ya Dunya Ya Gharami
Ya Law'ati
Ya Ma Banet Qasr El Amani
Ya Msafir Wahdak
X

Ya Nassia Waadi
Ya Shira'aan
Ya Tara Ya Nesma
Ya Wabour Ulli
Ya Ward Meen Yeshtireek
Yalli Futt El Mal Wil Gah
Yanaiman Raqadat Gofounuh
Zalamouni Ya Habibi
Zeina

Ahmed Adaweyah

Aham Aham
Bint El Sultan
Eilah Taihah
Elmarasi
Esah Rdah Embo
Etalemouha Baa'a
Habah Fouaa Wu Habah Taht
Kuloh Ala Kuloh
Salametha Om Hassan
Sib Wu Ana Asib
Zahmah

Other names of significance

Amr Diab
Asalah Nasri
Cheb Jilany
Diana Haddad
Diana Korazon
Ehab Tawfiq
Fadel Shaker
Fairouz
Fatme Serhan
George Wassouf
George Al-Rassi
Haifa Wahbe
Hakim
Hamada Helal
Hassan El Asmar
Hussein El Jassmy
Kazem El-Saher
Khaled Agaag

Latifa
Madonna
Mehlem Barakat
Nagwa Karam
Nancy Ajram
Nawal
Nawal El Zoughbi
Rico
Saad El Sughayar
Sabah
Saber El Robaey
Samara
Samira Saeed
Thekra
Wael Kfoury
Warda
Zekra

Chapter 15   The EDA Dance Notation System & Glossary

This glossary is an attempt to compile information to make it easier to look up, however - as dance and culture are intricate and neverending subjects - so is the work on completing this glossary.

Term	Abbreviation	Definition

A

Accent   (Acc)

dynamic movement created by contracting or releasing a muscle explosively.
1)   Folklore - *snap accent*, returns to neutral.
2)   Raqs Sharki - remains at the return point at end of execution.

Accents

1.   Static - muscular contraction, skeleton remains mainly in same position
2.   Dynamic - muscular contraction, skeleton follows
3.   Extending - muscular extension of body part
4.   Contacting - muscular contraction of body part
5.   Redirect - muscular change of direction
6.   Freeze - muscular accent with definite stop at return point of movement path
7.   Snap - muscular accent snapping back from return point of movement path

Aida Nour

former *Reda Troupe* member. World renown choreographer and dancer with a successful solo career as a Raqs Sharki dancer after the *Reda Troupe*. Specialized in 1940s style and has taught numerous dancers worldwide such as *Bahaia*, *Dandash* and many more. Innovative costumer and co-organizer of the Nile Group Festivals in Cairo, Egypt.

Appearance

see; *presentation*

Arabesque   (A)

extension of the leg, creating an extension from the finger tips to the toes

Asian Siccor Step   (ASS)

movement concept derived from the dances along the Silk Road consisting of scooting sideways alternating the weight on ball and heel.

Assaya

cane or staff used to dance *Saiidi* and execute *Tahtib*. Most often made of treated and processed Bamboo.

Assuit

Assuit items are made by hand hammering silver until it becomes flat and then it is used as a wide piece to make the designs in a net like fabric.

Assuyt	city in Upper Egypt.

Ayub
a 3/4 rhythm:
1 2 3
D T D T
Dum Tek Dum Tek

B

Bamboutaya
Egyptian folkdance from the Suez channel area and the channel cities. Other names; Port Said, Simsimayya, Egyptian Spoon dance

Bahrain
island kingdom in the Persian Gulf. Capital: Manama. Arabic; Ba'hrayn / Mamlakat al-Ba'hrayn

Balady
Arabic: the home country/countryside. Used in reference to an earthy, grounded dance style consisting of undulating and accenting movements increasing in strength and emphasis as the characteristic music starts out slow and escalades into a crescendo. Balady is an introvert Egyptian folk dance style with emphasize on being the musician's visual aid. This style has heavy undulation work as well as feeling incorporated with mostly stationary work. Just as balady music builds up from a beat to a crescendo of instruments, the dancer builds up his/her performance accordingly. Traditionally performed by women - Balady displays a non-commercial homage to the beauty of the female expression.

Balady
rhythm, see: *Masmoudi*

Barrel turn
see; *Vueltas Quebradas*

Bras, positions des (#)
positions of the arms

Body alignment
refers to the axis maintained in the body to achieve proper weight compensation when dancing based on 5 points; center foot, center calf, center thigh, center torso and center neck.

Bolero   bolero
Flamenco; 3 point turn. Consists of 1/2 turns or 180 degree turns on each count while stepping in the direction of movement on each turn creating a straight line from point A to point B. The feet are in 1 PdP on each step.

Breath count
refers to the count of movements or sequences that fit on a full breath, an inhale or an exhale. The breath should at all times remain calm and controlled and thereby provide a second nature count to the dancer. Mastering this concept provides extensive consistency in a dancer's work.

C

Camel	Camel	undulating movement generated in the abdomen
Chassé	Chassé	chased, A 3 count step where one foot chases the other (horse step / triplets)
Choreographer		Composer or inventor of dances
Choreography		the actual steps, grouping and patterns of a dance composition
Choo Choo shimmy	(ChooChoo)	movement concept consisting of generating a *shimmy* by gliding the working leg backward while the hip is aligned behind the weight point in the feet - rapidly alternating between the legs - creating a gliding illusion while the hip shimmies.
Conditioning		the sum of consistent practice in terms of injury prevention, strength, stamina, flexibility, body awareness, technical accuracy and quality of movement.
Corps, positions des	(PdC)	positions of the body
Croisé	(cross)	crossing of the legs/thighs
Cross pivot		see; *pirouette*

D

Dandash		acclaimed Egyptian dancer. Originally introduced as *Aida Nour*'s protegé.
Daraboukkah		drum
Debkeh		Folkdance genre from the Levant (Lebanon, Jordan, Palestine, Syria, Iraq). Characterized by display of athleticism, rapid foot work, shoulder work and dancing in lines.
Demi point	(relevé)	half toe/point
Demi plié	(folklore)	half bend of the knees
Demi tour	(DT)	half turn
Derrière	back	back
Devant	front	front

Dina		world renown Egyptian dancer. One of the first dancers from the famous *Reda Troupe* to revolutionize the stylization of Raqs Sharki in the early 1980s. Made famous by her risqué costuming, individual expression and stylization. Considered to be the trendsetter for numerous dancers worldwide.
Dina Sway	Dina Sway	movement concept directly derived from the Egyptian dancer Dina's stylization of a contained chest figure 8.
Double	(D)	double
Drop'n Kick	(DnK)	hip movement generated by a gliding up and down movement by the working hip and an accent on the supporting leg, and then a hip movement with a leg extension combined in various ways. Example: 1 x drop, 1 x drop with leg extension.

E

Egypt		country in North Africa bordering Jordan, Saudi Arabia, Israel, Libya, Sudan, the Mediterranean Sea and the Red Sea. Capital; Cairo. Arabic: Misr / Gumhuriyyet Masr el-'Arabiyyah
Entré	entrance	entrance
Étendu	(É)	outstretched, extended
Expression		the visual and emotional sum of *stylization*

F

Fallahi		1) Arabic; farmer
		2) Egyptian folkdance depicting everyday life as a farmer on the Egyptian countryside.
		3) a 2/4 rhythm. Fellahi means farmer or person from the countryside:

  1   2

D T | T D T

Dum Tek Tek Dum Tek

Faten Salama		former Kauomayya Troupe member currently based in Washington DC, USA and Cairo, Egypt. World renown for her strong and expressive Raqs Sharki style.
Flutter		Movement generated in the upper or lower abdomen by rapidly contracting or releasing the muscles

Fifi Abdou   One of the most acclaimed dancers and actresses in Egyptian history. Known as "Bint el Balad" - the daughter of the country and the dancer of the people. Originally from Alexandria, Fifi has had a long lasting career from the 1960s and is today considered to be one of the richest women in Cairo, the Egyptian capital. Famous for her Shaabi expression and authentic feel.

Figure 8   Fig 8   movement concept creating a figure 8 in a body part vertically, horizontally, backwards or forwards.

Finale   Finale   final section of a dance composition

Folklore hand   supported through the wrist and the thumb. The palm gently folds over the thumb and extends the fingers slightly downwards outside the thumb - fingertips aligning with the line created through the wrist and thumb. Fingers remain together, relaxed yet aware, at all times. There is an extension in the middle finger to maintain tension and awareness. The dancer will feel a tension in the flesh between the thumb and the palm as well contradicting the direction of the extension in the middle finger. NOTE: do not create a circular shape between the thumb and the index finger as this is a very rude hand gesture in several Middle Eastern and Asian cultures.

Fusion   a combination of 2 or more styles into a holistically merged expression preserving certain characteristics of each style resulting in a new innovative expression.

G

Gawazee   terminology used in reference to the folk dances that emerged in nomadic immigrant tribes to Egypt, i.e. Egyptian gypsies. Characterized by stomping movements, loose large hip movements and Zagat. Other names: Banat Mazin, Sonbati (reference to the names of families where stylization of specific Gawazee dance styles developed).

H

Hagallah   Hagallah   characteristic step for the North-Western Egyptian folkdance - Hagallah - an upbeat tribal folkdance from the Sinai areas of Egypt danced by un-wed women at social functions. Characteristic movements of this dance are immortalized all over the world through style specific vibrating and shimming movements.

Hip Circle   (HC)   4 or 8 count movement generated by leading the hip in a circle.

Hip Drop   (Hip down)   movement created by releasing the hamstring either slowly or dynamically.

I

Iraq   country bordering to Kuwait, Turkey, Iran, Jordan, Syria, Saudi Arabia and the Persian Gulf. Capital; Bagdad. Arabic; Iraq

Iraqi Khaleegi   EDA term used to describe the dance style of Southern Iraq and the Qawli people of Iraq. A combination of *Debkeh* influences and *Khaleegi* dance. Characterized by being upbeat and rapid along with the *Zambour*.

Iskanadarani   Arabic: from Alexandria. Refers to the fishermen's dances and the Melaya Leff style from the city of Alexandria.

Israel   country bordering to Egypt, Jordan, Palestine, Lebanon, Syria and the Mediterranean Sea. Capital; Tel Aviv. Arabic; Isra'il / Dawlat Isra'il

J

Jambe   (*)   leg

Jewel of the Nile   (Jewel)   movement concept characterized by the twisting of the hip.

Jordan   city in the Levant area bordering Lebanon, Saudi Arabia, Israel and Egypt. Capital; Amman. Arabic; Urdunn / Al-Mamlakah al-Urdunniyyah al-Hašimiyyah

K

Kanoun   see; Qanoun

Kauomayya Troupe   the National Folklore troupe of Egypt representing Egyptian culture internationally. Acclaimed dancers such as Freiz, *Lubna Emam*, *Faten Salama*, Ousama Emam and many more have their background in the Kauomayya Troupe. The stylization of the Kauomayya Troupe was established to be heavily folkloric in the expression and is more grounded than the Reda Troupe stylization due to the focus of the troupe's activities to be outside of Egypt and thus limited the level of innovation appropriate.

Khaleegi   1)   Arabic; from the Gulf, i.e. the Persian Gulf area. Used by dancers in reference to the dance styles Na'ashat and Samri - characterized by hair tosses, chest undulations, rotation of the hip and tight shoulder shimmies.

2)   a 4/4 rhythm and is characteristic of music from the Persian Gulf area:
1 2 3 4
D T D TT
Dum Tek Dum Tek Tek

Kuwait

country bordering the Persian Gulf, Saudi Arabia and Iraq. Capital; Kuwait City. Arabic; Kuwayt / Dawlat al-Kuwayt

L

Labanotation

dance notation system invented by Rudolf Von Laban, developed and perfected by the Dance Notation Bureau, NY

Lebanon

country in the Levant area boardering to Israel, Palestinian territories, Syria, Jordan and the Mediterranean Sea. Capital; Beirut.
Arabic; Lubnan / Al-Jumhuriyyah al-Lubnaniyyah

Levant

term used in reference to Israel, Jordan, Lebanon, Syria and the Palestinian territories.

Libya

country in North Africa bordering to Egypt, Sudan, Niger, Chad, Algeria, Tunisia and the Mediterranean Sea. Capital; Tripoli. Arabic; Libiyyah / Al-Jamahiriyyah al-`Arabiyyah al-Libiyyah aš-Ša`biyyah al-Ištirakiyyah al-`Udhma

Lower Egypt

term used in reference to the Nile delta area (north of modern day Cairo).

Lubna Emam

former Kauomayya Troupe member internationally recognized choreographer and instructor, especially recognized for her Khaleegi and Saiidi.

Lyrical layer

reflects the lyrics

M

Mahmoud Reda

the father of the stylization of Egyptian folklore and Raqs Sharki. Founder of the *Reda Troupe*. World renown choreographer and dancer. Researched the Egyptian folk dances and created an universal platform of technique and documented the characteristics of not only the dance styles themselves, but also the different regions, people and cultures of Egypt and incorporated this research into the stylization of the *Reda Troupe*. Former Olympic gymnast and Argentinean Tango dancer.

Mains, positions des (pdM)   positions of the hands

Malfouf   a 4/4 rhythm:
                               1   2
                               D T | T
                               Dum Tek Tek

Masmoudi   a 4/4 rhythm:
                               1   2   3   4
                               DD | T | D | TT
                               Dum Dum Tek(-e-tack) Dum Tek(-e-TekTek-e)

Here demonstrated with the Zagat pattern for the rhythm known to dancers as Balady in brackets.

Maya   (Fig 8 down) Figure 8 downwards generated in the hip.

Maqsoum   a 4/4 rhythm:
                               1 2 3 4
                               D | T D T
                               Dum Tek-e-tack-tack Dum Tek-e-tack

Melaya Leff   A character dance brought to fame by Mahmoud Reda and Fifi Abdou incorporating the modesty garment Melaya traditionally used in Egypt in the old days, but may still be seen worn in the poorer quarters of Cairo. The Melaya was brought to Egypt from Turkey during the reign of the Ottomans to preserve the modesty and decency of the women. White was worn by un-weds and black by wed women. The garment, however, showed great potential due to the fact that it could be tightened and loosened in strategic places, and so was the character dance Melaya Leff created. The Melaya character is tough, playful, strong and confident.

Melodic layer   reflects the melody line

Mizmar   wind instrument characteristic for folklore music especially for *Saiidi* and *Debkeh*. Different regions pitch their mizmar differently.

Movement count   refers to groups of technical counts and makes it easier to count numbers of movements in a sequence. Choreographies at the EDA are usually written in movement count in black.

Musical/Lyrical count   refers to the lyrical image of the music and ensures accuracy in the dancer's expression and timing.

N

Notation		a system of recording dance compositions in writing - dance notation. The EDA operates by it's own constructed dance notation system - the EDA Dance Notation System, EDA DNS™.

O

Oblique		vertical side muscles in the abdominal and waist area
Oman		country on the Saudi Arabian peninsula bordering Saudi Arabia, Yemen, UAE, the Persian Gulf, the Gulf of Oman and the Arabian Sea. Capital; Muscat. Arabic; 'Uman / Saltanat 'Uman
Opposition	(O)	engaging and activating diagonal body parts in a sequence
Oriental(e)		refers to the classical style of Raqs Sharki
Oud		a musical instrument of the Middle East and northern Africa belonging to the lute family.

P

Paddle turn		refers to the way Sufi dancers (i.e. Whirling Dervishes and Tanoura dancers) keep their weight focused on one leg while "paddling" around the leg with the other leg.
Palestine		territories consisting of the Gaza strip, the West Bank and the Golan Heights in the Levant areas bordering to Israel, Lebanon, Egypt, Syria, Jordan and the Mediterranean Sea. Arabic; Filas'tin, Falas'tin, Filis'tin.
Pas de Bourrée	(PdB)	bourrées are usually tiny running steps in which the feet are kept close together. They are most often performed in relevée and can travel in any direction
Pas de Deux	(PdD)	dance for two
Passé	Passé	passed, the foot of one leg passes the knee of the supporting leg
Pieds, Positions des	(PdP)	positions of the feet
Pirouette	(P)	whirl/spin with spotting. Consists of 2 counts. On the first count the supporting leg pushes off the floor and transfers the weight onto the active leg. The force of the push turns the body around with the active leg as the center and pivoting. On the second count the body returns to default

position and the weight transfers back to the supporting leg.
Cross pirouette; refers to the fact that the dancers legs/feet cross prior to executing the turn. There are various weight distribution concepts and concepts of crossing and pivoting in this type of turns. A great alternative.

Pivot turn — see; *pirouette*

Plat, à — flat — on the feet

Port de Bras — (Pd#) — arm paths

Presentation — the visual and artistic sum of costuming, make up, hair, music, face, stylization and technical skill level.

O

Qanoun — musical instrument of North Africa and Middle East known as the Zither in the west.

Qatar — country on the Saudi Arabian peninsula bordering the Persian Gulf and Saudi Arabia. Capital; Doha. Arabic; Qatar / Dawlat Qatar

Quatrième, À la — (4th) — fourth position Ballet of the body

R

Randa Kamel — acclaimed Egyptian dancer considered to be the new trendsetter after *Dina*. Former *Reda Troupe* member and known for her innovative style along with incomparable strength.

Raqia Hassan — former member of the *Reda Troupe*. Today world renown choreographer and trendsetter for the worldwide dance scene of Raqs Sharki through own teachings and through given instruction to recognized names such as *Dina, Randa Kamel, Zahra Zuhair, Jillina* and more. Organizer of the Ahlan Wa Sahlan festival in Cairo.

Raqs Assaya — see; *Saiidi*

Raqs Sharki — Arabic: dance from the east. Refers to the classical expression of Egyptian dance, i.e. Egyptian belly dance. Ra's Sharki - Bellydance - from Egypt is often known as Egyptian style. The style is based on Egyptian folkloric dances as well as influences from Ballet, Asian dances and western dances. The dance form combines fluid movements with sharp precise accents along with multiple layers of movements giving an amazing and impressive display of muscular control. This through the concepts of resistance, release, containment and force incorporated in the movements. Different styles are Classical Raqs Sharki - used for classical musical pieces, Modern Raqs Sharki - used for more modern pieces, Cabaret - used for nightclub settings. Raqs Sharki takes influences from all folkdances of Egypt depending on the expression of the music utilized. The more modern styles take influences from Jazz, Modern, Ballet, HipHop, Street and other dances. Most musical pieces are instrumental, however - classical pieces may have highly poetic vocals incorporated whereas the dancer's cultural understanding as well as ability to express the full musical and lyrical aspect of the music is displayed. Traditionally danced by women, but today the art form also embraces male performers. Throughout the times there have been periods where young male dancers were dressed up as women and entertained instead of female dancers due to social, religious or legal restrictions towards female dancers. Male dancers otherwise mostly did folkdances. As the art of Raqs Sharki reached the Western world, the art of male Raqs Sharki - with male performers dressed as men - evolved and has become a widely accepted phenomenon. Highly acknowledged dancers, instructors and choreographers of Raqs Sharki are male and they contribute to promote, preserve and evolve the dance with their fellow female colleagues. The art of Male Raqs Sharki is new and leaves room for individual interpretation and influences in each performer's style.

Raqs Sharki hand

based upon the folklore hand. The thumb is placed against the outside of the first joint of the middle finger from the palm. The index finger is extended above the thumb, the ring finger is aligned with the index finger on the opposite side of the middle finger and the pinky extends slightly above the ring finger. There is an extension in the middle finger to maintain tension and awareness. The dancer will feel a tension in the flesh between the thumb and the palm as well contradicting the direction of the extension in the middle finger. NOTE: do not create a circular shape between the thumb and the index finger as this is a very rude hand gesture in several Middle Eastern and Asian cultures.

Reda Troupe

dance troupe established in the 1960s by Mahmoud Reda setting the standard for stylization of Egyptian folklore worldwide. A stylization considered to be the forerunner for the current standard of stylization of Egyptian Raqs Sharki. The stylization has a clear Balletic quality and influence. Names such as Aida Nour, Dandash, Dina, Farida Fahmy, Raqia Hassan, Yousry Sharif and many many more all have background in the Reda Troupe.

Relevée	(Rel)	raised
Repetition	(REP)	rehearsal/repeat/practice
Riqq		Arabic; tamourine
Rond	(R)	round/circular
Rond de Bras	(RdB)	circular motion of the arms

Rond de Jambe	(RdJ)	circular motion of the leg
Rhythmic count		refers to the rhythmic count as presented in the previous lesson. This ensures accuracy in the dancer's technique and movements when it comes to following the rhythmic image of the music.
Rhythmic layer		reflects the rhythm

S

Saiidi		1. term describing a person from Al-Saiid.
		2. Egyptian folk dance often danced with cane(s) or staff(s). Characterized by earthy, grounded movements, shoulder and heel bounces and twirling of the cane(s) or staff(s). Emulates the movements of a dancing horse. Derived from the martial art form of *Tahtib*. Traditionally done by men. Female version involves hip work and is referred to as *Raqs Assaya* - dance of the cane.
		3. Saiidi is 4/4 rhythm and is characteristic for music from Upper Egypt (south): 1 2 3 4 D T | DD T Dum Tek Dum Dum Tek
Saiidi hop	Saiidi hop	movement concept consisting of a bending of the knees while feet are together, a pivot on the weighted leg along with a downward heel bounce while the un-weighted leg extends through the air.
Saiidi Step	Saiidi Step	movement concept consisting of a step and a heel bounce on the working leg while the supporting leg extends or lifts.
Samaii		a 10/8 rhythm and is characteristic for Anadalusian music: 1 2 3 4 5 6 7 8 9 10 D | | T | | DD | T Dum Tek Dum Dum Tek
Samia	Samia	movement concept named after the golden Era dancer and actress Samia Gamaal consisting of an accent, then shimmy-series.
Samia Gamaal		renown dancer and actress from the 1940s.
Saudi Arabia		country on the Saudi Arabian peninsula bordering the Persian Gulf, UAE, Bahrain, Kuwait, Qatar, Oman, Yemen, Jordan, Iraq, Egypt and the Red Sea. Capital; Riyadh. Arabic; Saudi / Al-Mamlaka al-'Arabiyya as-Sa'udiyya

Seconde, À la	(2nd)	second position Ballet of the body
Sequence count		refers to groups of movement counts and makes it easier to block out sequences in repetitions. Repetitions ensure familiarity with the material both for the dancer and the audience. Choreographies at the EDA are usually written with sequence counts in gray.
Shaabi		Arabic; Sha'abi - meaning "(of) the people" - is a playful and flirtatious dance style with influences from the street dances of Mohammed Ali Street in Cairo and the village dancers in the Egyptian country side. This powerful and fun style allows the dancers to display their acting skills as well as versatility within expressions. Styles within Shaabi would be Folklore style, Urban style and Cabaret style - as well as local variations within the style. Shaabi is at times performed with Zagat (finger cymbals).
Shimmy	(shimmy)	movement generated by contracting the oppositing muscles on the sides of the body continuously
Snake arms	snake arms	arm undulation
Snap accent		see; *accent*
Spotting	(Sp)	movement of the head/eyes in turns. The head is the last to leave and first to arrive at the focal point chosen. Often use to prevent dizziness.
Step	(Step)	transition of weight from one leg to the other
Step Step Arabesque	(SSA)	movement concept based on *Step Step Arabesque*.
Stretching		loosening, limbering of the muscles. Détiré
Stylistic layer		reflects the style of the dance
Stylization		to design in or cause to conform to a particular style, as of representation or treatment in art; conventionalize. Often achieved through consistency in arms, positioning, character, intent and emphasis in movement. *(Random House Unabridged Dictionary, © Random House, Inc. 2006.)*
Suheir Zaki		1. Egyptian dancer famous for having been the first dancer to ever dance to Oum Kalthoum's music. Called the Oum Kalthoum of dance by Oum Kalthoum herself.
	(Zaki)	2. movement concept derived from Suheir Zaki's stylization of Raqs Sharki consisting of a downward hip accent on the weighted leg.
Supporting leg	(SL)	versus working leg. The supporting leg supports the body and initiates a movement while the working leg is freed up to execute given movement
Syria		country bordering to Turkey, Iraq, Jordan, Lebanon, Palestine, Israel and the Mediterranean Sea. Capital; Damascus. Arabic; Suriyah / Al-Jumhuriyyah al-?Arabiyyah as-Suriyyah

T

Tahtib

Egyptian martial arts form performed with staffs and canes. Often executed as a duel.

Tanoura

Tanoura is the Egyptian version of the Whirling Dervish dances of the Sufis (Islamic mysticism). Due to the spiritual and religious aspect of this dance, and out of respect for the same, the EDA avoids the usage of corresponding music and dances. However the techniques and concepts of the styles are addressed and utilized partially in music of other styles that has influences of Tanoura.

Tanoura turn

see; *paddle turn*

Technical count

refers to the count a movement is build up by. Each count refers to a certain part of the movement at a certain place/time in the movement. This ensures consistency in the technique and makes it easier to identify where in the technical count layering occurs. Also, technical count enables the dancer to synchronize various counts in different layers together.

Tour   (T)

turn

Traditionalism

1.   strict adherence to traditional methods or teachings
2.   adherence to tradition (especially in cultural or religious matters)
3.   the doctrine that all knowledge was originally derived by divine revelation and that it is transmitted by traditions
   (*WordNet® 3.0, © 2006 by Princeton University.*)
4.   EDA; folklore movements or stylization created or established throughout time.

Transitions   (PS)

1.   passing - where one body part passes another

(X)
2.   crossing - where one body part crosses the path of another

(redir)
3.   redirecting - where a body part executes a movement redirecting the direction of the body

(cont)
4.   continuing - where a body part continues on to the next position

Turn-out   (TO)

the ability of the dancer to turn feet and legs out from the hip joints to a 90 degree position - en-dehors

U

UAE

United Arab Emirates, coalition of 7 emirates (Abu Dhabi, Ajman, Dubai,

Fujairah, Ras al-Khaimah, Sharjah, and Umm al-Quwain) on the Saudi Arabian Peninsula and bordering the Persian Gulf, Saudi Arabia and Oman. Capital: Abu Dabhi.

Ummi	ummi	circular horizontal movement created through series of contractions and releases in the obliques

Undulation   undulation

1. flowing movement in region of body as per further specification
2. abdominal movement generated through alternatively contracting and releasing the abs.

Upper Egypt   term used in reference to the southern part of Egypt. Called "upper" due to the direction of the flow of the Nile river starting in Uganda and Ethiopia, and entering the southern part of Egypt through Sudan - flowing into the Mediterranean Sea in the northern part of Egypt and the city of Alexandria. Defined as south of modern day Cairo.
Lower Egypt; the Nile delta.

V

Veil   a 6 or 8 feet long fabric used as a lyrical instrument by the dancer. May be any fabric, but is traditionally made of Chiffon or Silk.

Vueltas Quebradas   Flamenco; barrel turns. Common in Flamenco and Classical Indian dance and refers to the above head arm position the dancer traditionally keeps while executing a Bolero turn in place along with a torso / back bend. It gives the illusion that the dancer's upper body and arms are "stuck" in a barrel while the dancer turns. Thereof the name Barrel turns.

W

Wahed wa Nous   (WWN)   Arabic; one and a half. Refers to number of steps taken in the concept of WWN.

Warm-up   exercise done to prevent injuries in muscles and tendons and to prepare for strenuous activity

Working leg   (WL)   executes movements

Y

Yemen   country on the Saudi Arabian peninsula boardering Oman, Saudi Arabia, the Red Sea and the Arabian Sea. Capital; Sanaa. Arabic; Yamaniyaah / Al-Jumhuriyyah al-Yamaniyyah

Yousry Sharif

former *Reda Troupe* member renown for his master *Tahtib* and *Saiidi* technique. World acclaimed choreographer and dancer. Today established in New York and owner of the Egyptian Dance Academy. World reknown for his innovative and modern take on Raqs Sharki and ability to embody the music in new ways.

Z

Zaar

1) Zaar is an Egyptian spiritual dance used to exorcise evil spirits. Due to the spiritual and religious aspect of this dance, and out of respect for the same, the EDA avoids the usage of corresponding music and dances. However the techniques and concepts of the styles are addressed and utilized partially in music of other styles that has influences of Zaar.

2) a 2/4 rhythm and is characteristic for exorcisms:
1   2
D T D T
Dum Tek Dum Tek

Zaffa

1) Zaffa is traditionally danced when an Egyptian wedding is announced and the bride is taken from her parents' house and delivered at the groom's residence. The dance is often danced with large candelabras known as Shamadan balanced on the head. Zaffa is traditionally a women's dance. A Shamadan dance has evolved from the tradition of Zaffa through the work of Mahmoud Reda and is often danced in groups.

2) Zaffa is a 4/4 rhythm characteristic for wedding processions:
1   2   3 4
D T D T D TT
Dum Tek Dum Tek Dum Tek Tek

Zagat

element

Arabic; finger cymbals. Also referred to as Zills (Turkish). Percussive folklore instrument used by the dancer to acknowledge the folklore to the music. Also used to show technical skill level and ability to multitask. Played in various rhythm patterns either to compliment an already existing percussive rhythm in the music or to add another percussive instrument and create a more interesting sound picture.

Zambour

a slender drum one headed percussive instrument only found in Iraq and sounds like a machine gun.

Chapter 16 References

Bibliography

Al Mashriq.no

a primer for movement description; Cecily Dell. ISBN 0-932582-03-6

Ballet for Dummies; Scott Speck & Evelyn Cisneros. ISBN 0-7645-2568-9

Basic Principles of Classical Ballet; Agrippina Vaganova. ISBN 0-486-22038-2

Dictionary.com:
WordNet® 3.0, © 2006 by Princeton University
Random House Unabridged Dictionary, © Random House, Inc. 2006

Din Personliga Tränare; Matt Roberts. ISBN 91-973429-8-X

Fitness för Honom; Kim Justin. ISBN91-973943-5-1

Gymnos; Asbjørn Gjerset, Kjell Haugen, Per Holmstad, Raghnild Lied. ISBN 82-02-13612-1

Jeremiah Soto

Practical weight training; Kevin Pressley. ISBN 0-7525-1025-1074-6

Real Men Do Yoga; John Capouya. ISBN 0-7573-0112-6

Styrketräning; Frédéric Delavier. ISBN 91-974146-7-0

Technical Manual And Dictionary of Classical Ballet; Gail Grant. ISBN 0-486-21843-0

The Compleat Belly Dancer; Julie Russo Mishkin & Marta Schill. ISBN 0-385-03556-X

The Complete Book of Yoga; Sri Ananda. ISBN 81-222-0094-X

The Genius of Flexibility; Bob Cooley. ISBN 0-7432-7087-8

The Music of the Arabs; Habib Hassan Touma. ISBN 1-57467-081-6

The Ultimate Guide to Weight Traning for Cheerleading; Robert G. Price. ISBN 1-932549-05-6

Yoga; Patricia A. Ralston and Caroline Smart. ISBN 0-06-073429-9

Wikipedia.org

Ät, träna, prestera; Fredrik Paulún. ISBN 91-973943-1-9
XVIII

The EDA Hierarchy

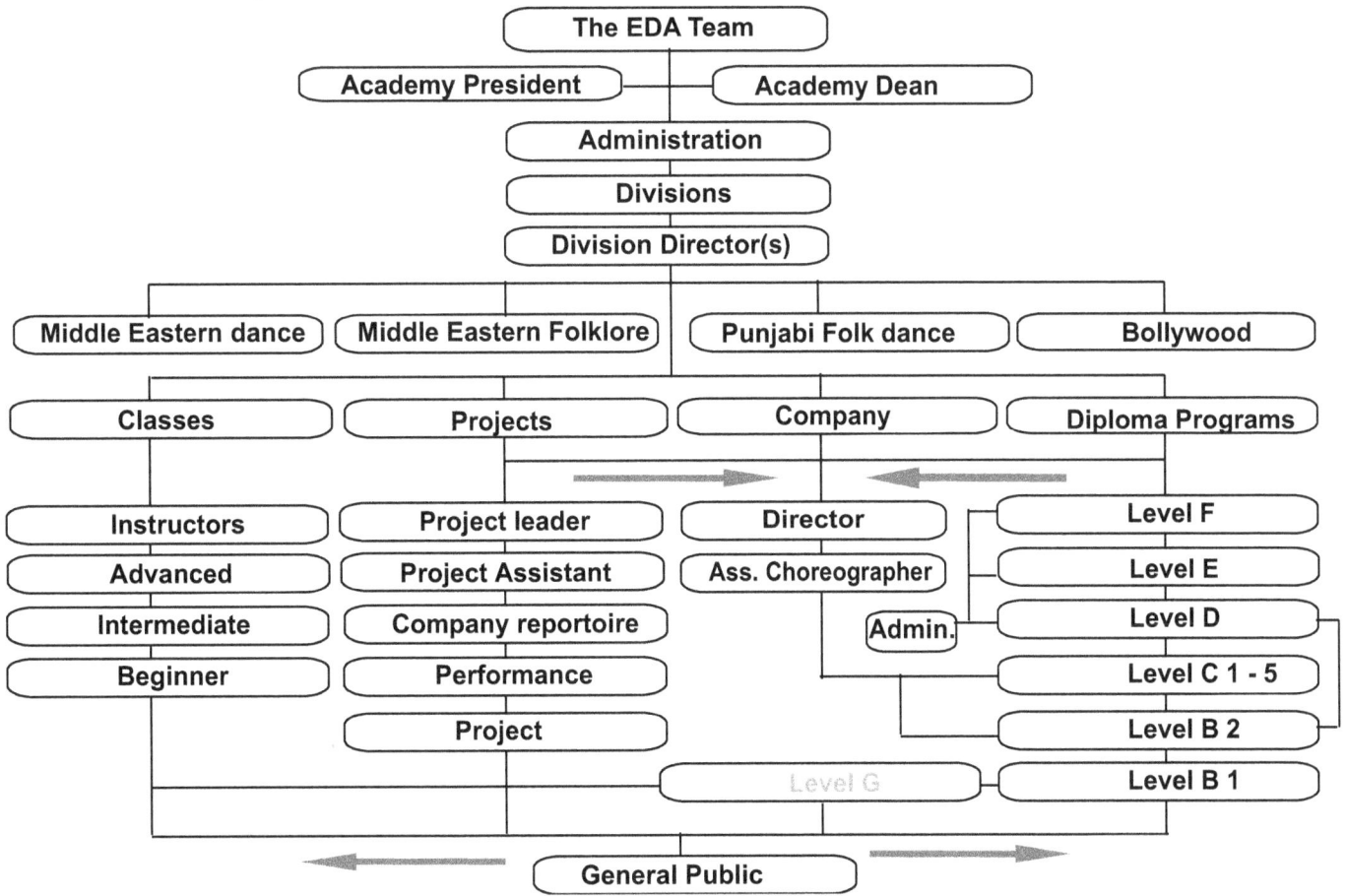

```
                          The EDA Team
        Academy President ─────── Academy Dean
                         Administration
                           Divisions
                      Division Director(s)

Middle Eastern dance   Middle Eastern Folklore   Punjabi Folk dance   Bollywood

      Classes              Projects              Company          Diploma Programs

    Instructors         Project leader          Director             Level F
     Advanced          Project Assistant     Ass. Choreographer      Level E
    Intermediate      Company reportoire         Admin.              Level D
     Beginner           Performance                                Level C 1 - 5
                          Project                                   Level B 2
                                            Level G                 Level B 1

                          General Public
```

Other EDA Products

The EDA offers a series of apparel, bags and more. Check it out at www.cafepress.com/the_eda

www.ingramcontent.com/pod-product-compliance
Lightning Source LLC
Chambersburg PA
CBHW081155090426
42736CB00017B/3339